POLLYWOGS
and
SHELLBACKS
Afloat

Aurora

P&O Cruises *Aurora* – 76,000 tons 1,870 Passengers, 850 Officers and Crew.

Two night to twenty-five night cruises to the Mediterranean, the Baltic & the Fjords, the Atlantic Isles, the Caribbean and Round the World cruising.

Patricia Carlton

POLLYWOGS and SHELLBACKS *Afloat*

PLANKTON BOOKS
HASLEMERE • SURREY

POLLYWOGS
and
SHELLBACKS
Afloat

First published in the UK in 2005 by
PLANKTON BOOKS
Manesty, Weydown Road, Haslemere, Surrey GU27 1DR

ISBN 0-9551163-0-9 (10-digit **ISBN**)

ISBN 978-0-9551163-0-8 (13-digit **ISBN**)

Produced and printed by members of
THE GUILD OF MASTER CRAFTSMEN

Cover Design by Ian Tyrrell
Book Design and Typesetting by Cecil Smith
Typeset in New Baskerville

Printed and bound in Great Britain by
RPM PRINT & DESIGN
2-3 Spur Road, Quarry Lane, Chichester, West Sussex PO19 8PR

For HIMSELF
My darling husband Greg,
without whom none of this would
have been possible

ACKNOWLEDGEMENTS

With sincere thanks to Felicity who began as my creative writing
tutor and became my friend, without whose encouragement this
book would never have been written. To Cilla and Alex who
painstakingly corrected my dyslexic spellings and punctuation and
to Malcolm who returned my manuscript with a plethora of
Post-its® – many of his suggestions have been incorporated.
Special thanks to First Officer Neil Turnbull, now Staff Captain
Neil Turnbull, who arranged the tour 'below stairs' and
Captain Ian Walters who never failed to steer *Aurora* safely in
calm waters throughout the cruise.
And finally, grateful thanks to the ever-helpful Cruise Options
who kindly gave me sponsorship towards the publication
of this book.

CONTENTS

1

ALL ABOARD

One week to go, and counting!

I've been like this ever since I turned the page on the calendar from April to May. As usual, I'm not just looking forward to it; I'm beside myself with excitement. The nearer we get, the more slowly the hours seem to pass. Each night, after I've put the light off, I lie in bed and think about it. Mentally, I'm there already. It doesn't matter that I've done it before and know exactly what will happen, because each one is different, each one brings its own special excitement, and each one will leave its own wonderful memories. But by the memory stage, I'll be thinking about the next one!

I have become a Cruise-oholic.

No! You won't find it in the dictionary, but it's what you become when you love cruising as much as I do and, like me, you'd prefer to feel the motion of the ship beneath your feet rather than immovable, solid ground. I've become a pushover, an easy-touch. I'm not proud! Offer me a cruise and I'll go. I won't think twice as to

1

where the ship will visit. I won't query what the weather will be like, or the temperature. It won't even bother me which ship I'm going on or what I'll find on board. I'll just happily grab my suitcases, fling in a few favourite holiday clothes, a couple of must-read books, and slam the door behind me with hardly a second thought.

In all the cruises Himself and I have been on, I have yet to remember one with anything but happiness.

* * * * *

But it wasn't always like this. We haven't always taken this wonderfully relaxing option. We've had our fair share of airport queues, screaming children (often our own) and delayed flights. We've paid for excess baggage, retrieved delayed baggage and mourned over lost baggage. We've endured airline food, and been squeezed up against the passenger from hell in the next seat. They've chatted to us when we wanted to sleep and we've wished they'd wake up when we wanted to go to the loo. We've climbed off endless aircraft resembling the crumpled dregs of the laundry basket.

But now, you see, I'm past it. Correction! We're past it. Himself and I, we don't do airports any longer, where you often have to walk for miles. We don't appreciate starting a holiday with a long wait for a flight. And who does enjoy the endless hours packed into a flying sardine can?

Throughout any holiday by air, the thought of the return flight hangs overhead like a large jumbo jet.

"Don't buy that. We won't be able to carry it home."

"Our flight doesn't leave until 02.00 I wonder if they'll let us keep our room?"

"Look! Today's flight is arriving." This comment is

shouted above the noise of the jet as it screams down the flight path towards the airport whose perimeter fence appears to be next to the swimming pool.

And if you don't like your destination, you do have choices. You can endure it and return home muttering about your disappointing holiday, or change hotels. In the worst-case scenario, you can even catch the next sardine can home.

These days we choose to take a more leisurely option.

* * * * *

Some time back in September last year, Himself passed the P&O brochure to me and said: "This one looks good. We can visit Enzo whilst we're in Rome."

"And I can buy some more earrings in Gibraltar."

"And I'll have my birthday on board," Himself added, no doubt remembering other birthday celebrations we've seen on previous cruises.

"How about lunch in Florence this time?"

"You're on. Shall I book the cruise?"

"Need you ask?"

"Well there's always the chance you'd rather not go!"

"Not when there's a ship involved," I grinned, handing back the brochure as he went off to make a telephone booking.

* * * * *

But that was last autumn and between then and now we've been on another cruise, returning home just before Christmas. I wasn't joking when I told you I was a Cruise-oholic.

OK. So Himself is now retired and I'm no longer a

teenager, but that doesn't mean you have to be in our state of decay to go on a cruise. Married couples and singles of all ages – toddlers to teenagers – babies to slightly bewildered wrinklies – pushchairs to Zimmer frames – roller-skates to wheelchairs and golf clubs to bicycles. On board the ship we will be travelling on, we'll find the lot.

And in the unlikely event that the itinerary has a port that you don't want to visit, you can always stay on board. No one will force you to take in the delights of Rome, eat pasta in Florence, visit the shops in Barcelona, or take pictures of the wild life in Gibraltar. There is always the joy of the nearly empty ship to keep you occupied. Have a facial or a massage in the beauty salon, watch a film in the cinema, read a book in the library, eat too much in any of the restaurants, or just become a sun-bed-slug and soak up the sunshine.

But there is much, much more to cruising than the ports as you'll see the further you go into this book. In fact the longer you cruise, the more incidental the ports are and there comes a time when they almost become an unnecessary and irritating interruption to the relaxed life on board.

On a recent cruise, one of the ship's officers was talking to me about his idea of having a fortnights' cruise... to nowhere! It would leave Southampton, steam off down the Channel and return two wonderful relaxing weeks later, having visited... the Atlantic Ocean or maybe the Mediterranean, or possibly the coast of Norway so you'd have had the occasional glimpse of some rugged mountains and fjords disappearing inland. What a wonderful cruise that would be... for me! I can't think of anything better, although Himself wouldn't agree, and so for now we'll have to enjoy some ports of call.

Right! You have just one week before we cast off. One week to gather together some easy-to-wear clothes for the days spent on board the ship or when you go on shore, and some smarter clothes for the evenings. Add a couple of outfits for formal occasions, a dinner jacket or dark suit for the gentlemen, some suntan lotion, sunglasses and a book or two. Don't forget to stop the milk, cancel the papers and then you can jump into your transport for your journey to the docks.

* * * * *

Great excitement. It's Saturday. The suitcases are down from the roof and looking forlornly empty, lying on the bed waiting to be filled. On the side sits a pile of items I can't possibly do without on my holidays – despite the fact I know that half of them will be brought back unused. There is no weight limitation on this holiday! If you feel like taking the kitchen sink, then you can do so, but mind how you pack the taps! Shoes, swimwear, and a sunhat; trousers, tops and my teddy bear... oh yes I do! Camera, cardigan and Himself's cufflinks. Don't forget your passport, tickets, travellers' cheques and cash. You can buy foreign currency on board if you wish, and also change travellers' cheques at reception.

It's time for bed. All our packing is finished. The suitcases have their labels tied on firmly, and all that remains is a good night's sleep before making our way to Southampton where our luxurious floating hotel awaits.

* * * * *

Embarking passengers see the beautiful ship *Aurora* long before they arrive at the quayside. She towers above the dock buildings and can easily be seen from the flyover on the road into Southampton. It never fails to give me a thrill as I shout: "Ship ahoy! There she is. Oh good, she's facing the right way. Our cabin will be overlooking the quayside so we can hear the band playing as we leave."

Have you forgotten anything? Don't worry if you have done as most items can be bought on board in the well-stocked shops – everything from a nail file to a dinner jacket, shorts and pedal pushers to Pringles. You can buy books, postcards and presents for those at home. There really is no need to get off this floating hotel. And at the end of the cruise, you can even buy an expandable travel bag on board in which you can pack all those souvenirs you've bought during the holiday.

Having arrived at the terminal building, don't get worried as your suitcases are whisked out of sight. The next time you see them, they'll be in your cabin. What could be easier than that? Walk in through the entrance over there and take your tickets to the desk. The ladies will need to see your passport, you'll be handed your cruise card, which you must carry for the duration of the cruise, and then just wait in the departure lounge until your boarding card number is called. Enjoy a cup of coffee or have a drink, buy a last minute magazine or possibly make friends with the couple you're sitting next to – you're sure to see them on board at some stage.

And finally, it's time to relax! It is all over! The hassle of the journey is now behind you. You're about to go on board *Aurora* at the start of a wonderful trip to the Mediterranean. Whilst your next-door neighbours, who are flying off to Spain for a holiday, are still stuck on the M25 or in the queue at the airport, you are about to walk onto your luxurious hotel. Don't forget to smile –

you never know who might be about to take your photograph! See you on board.

* * * * *

A life on the ocean waves, hey diddle de dum de dum… We're afloat! We have just cast off, and are actually leaving Southampton at this moment. The sun is smiling happily upon us through the open balcony door and paper streamers from our departure celebrations (biodegradable of course) are blowing across my view, caught on the rails of that balcony. I grab some streamers of blue, red, yellow and white – colours of the company owning this wonderful ship. The sounds of the Central Band of The Royal British Legion, who played as we slowly moved away from the quayside, are still ringing inside my head.

I sing, somewhat out of tune, "We are sailing, we are sailing", and then, because I can't remember the words, I repeat, and repeat, "we are sailing, we ARE sailing!" much to the annoyance of Himself who shakes his head, but at the same time smiles at my obvious happiness.

A short while later, and we've eaten our canapés – caviar today – and have our complimentary champagne well under way… which is what we are too… well under way. Calm seas, a gentle breeze, the sun now sleepily heading towards the horizon – we're under way on the P&O cruise ship *Aurora*. Named after the goddess of the Dawn, she is heading for the Mediterranean on a cruise that will take two glorious weeks.

Tomorrow, by the time we're all eating breakfast, we'll be in the Bay of Biscay and steadily steaming towards our first port of call. There are 76,000 tons of luxury floating hotel beneath my bottom as I relax on the settee and listen to the squawking of a seagull. He peers in through the open door as he floats past, caught momentarily in the slipstream of this magnificent ship. Happy? You bet! The stress of land-based life has melted away as each mile has floated past, fading with every mouthful of bubbles, which are now tickling my nose.

"Do you think in an earlier life I had webbed feet?" I ask my equally relaxed husband, who is now horizontal and reading the Sunday papers. After this, the only newspaper he will read for 14 days will be the small one printed on board and delivered daily to our cabin.

"Or maybe fins?" I carry on. "Perhaps I was a mermaid with blonde hair and a long, green, scaly tail!"

Was that a snore?

I raise my glass in his direction and quietly add, "I hope you have a wonderful cruise my darling," before I go and sit on the balcony.

A guy in a motorboat is speeding past us, his passengers waving madly to anyone inclined to wave back – and we do; cruise passengers are a friendly lot! The Solent is heaving with tiny boats, ferries between the mainland and the Isle of Wight, the odd buoy, and a water skier who seems to be attached to a parachute! You do see life on board a cruise ship.

* * * * *

But we've missed a bit – let's wind the clock back a few hours.

Southampton, and the Mayflower Terminal for P&O's departures! This is the Embarkation and Disembarkation Day, or turn around day. The logistics of getting the passengers on and off the ship cause a massive headache for any cruise company. Today there are up to 1,870 passengers to process, every one of whom wants to get on board *immediately*!

Few of us care to remember that *Aurora* only docked at around 07.00 this morning from her last cruise, ten days to Madeira and the Canaries. From the moment she tied up at the terminal, life has been frantic for everyone concerned. Approximately the same number of passengers disembarked by 11.00 and retrieved their luggage from where it had been placed in cabin deck order in the baggage hall. Then, with much hugging and kissing goodbye of new friends, they all walked through the Customs Hall and connected with their varying forms of transport – cars, coaches, taxis – and departed.

Some of the crew too will have come to the end of their contract period and left the ship, and their replacements will have arrived during the day. The stores for the next cruise will be loaded on board and the stewards will be cleaning and re-organising the cabins for the new passengers who are now sitting impatiently in the Departure Lounge. This tight schedule will apply even before *Aurora* starts her 80 day world cruise in January. Cruise ships are like aircraft. An aircraft on the ground doesn't earn money for the company, and the same applies to a cruise ship. A quick turn round is in everyone's interests. After all, who wants to linger in dock in Southampton when the delights of the Mediterranean await?

We've checked in our cruise tickets, been given our cruise cards, which will act like a credit card whilst we're on board *Aurora*, and now have our boarding passes which will gain us entry onto the ship.

However, there is one further formality before we are allowed to go on board *Aurora* and start our holiday –

our first official ship's photograph. I always feel somewhat foolish, dressed in travel clothes, vanity case in one hand, laptop computer in the other, handbag over one shoulder. I'm trying not to drop my sun hat, and at the same time making sure Himself doesn't trip over anything. At this point, you know you're almost on board as you're asked to "stop on that line", and barely given time to smile, before the flash goes off in your face. You have probably just had your worst photograph taken on the cruise – it can only get better from this point. I will add that the best photograph Himself and I ever had taken was on board a ship, so don't despair when you view it tomorrow in the Photo Gallery, and after all, you don't have to buy it!

Of course, you can escape this whole procedure by smiling and firmly saying "no thank you," but why not enter into the spirit of the holiday at this point? You are here to enjoy yourself and the photograph will show just how tired and drawn you looked on Embarkation Day. It will also show the dates of the cruise and the ports you will be visiting. The more you cruise, and I hope you'll become dedicated cruisers like the majority of today's passengers, the more these 'Welcome Aboard' photographs become important in your life. They are useful when trying to settle arguments at home as to where you went, on which ship and in what year. One cruise does tend to merge with another with very little effort, as you'll see.

But never mind all the queues, the x-ray machines, the walk along the covered walkways, we are now on board, and for some of you this will be your first cruise. You can tell it's the start of the cruise as there are two sorts of passengers. Those who have been on board before, and those who are already wide-eyed and open mouthed at the size and splendour of this very modern cruise ship. Some are showing off their knowledge of the layout of the ship, whilst others are wandering around, a small cross-sectional plan of the ship in their hands, desperately searching for afternoon tea.

"Which is the front?" obviously a new passenger asks.

Another looks puzzled as she gazes at her cross sectional plan. "I'm trying to find Reception. Have I got this map the correct way round?" I point her in the right direction, and just in time stop myself from saying, "I hope so, or we'll be like the *Titanic* and sink!" – cruise passengers are a bit touchy about the 'T' word!

"See you in Charlie's for a glass of bubbly before dinner." Clearly a seasoned sailor doing his little bit of showing off!

Before we go any further I should explain a few things as we are being shown to our cabin by one of the stewards. We, and that includes you, are doing this cruise in real style. We have a suite on the starboard side – that is on the right hand side of the ship when facing the bow or front. And, because you'll need to know when the Officer of the Watch announces from the Bridge, "Dolphins on the Port side", the port side is the other side of the ship. For those of you on your first cruise, why not travel in luxury? Let's enjoy one of the best suites that *Aurora* can offer – complete with a Butler! There are cabins on board to suit all budgets and a study of a cruise brochure will supply details of the accommodation available.

Bing Bong... you'll soon get used to this noise as it heralds an announcement over the intercom. "Ladies and Gentlemen. At 16.30 there will be a Passenger General Emergency Station Drill and it is mandatory that all passengers who joined the ship in Southampton attend this drill." The voice from the Bridge breaks into our quiet cabin.

"On hearing the Emergency Signal of seven short blasts and one long blast on the ship's whistle over the ship's public address system, you should put on warm clothing, a head covering and proceed to your Muster Station carrying your life jacket. Remember to take any medication that you are currently using. If for any reason you are unable to return to your cabin, then proceed directly to your Muster Station, where a life jacket will be provided for you."

"A Muster Station is a place of safety, usually a lounge, theatre or similar place, where passengers are gathered together in the case of an emergency. A plan showing directions to *your* Muster Station can be found on the back of your cabin door."

I glance at my watch – 16.20 – time to wake Himself and proceed to our Muster Station. From the top shelf of our wardrobe, I collect our life jackets – bright orange – I never wear orange – the colour does absolutely nothing for me!

* * * * *

Barely pausing in mid-snore, Himself and I are now sitting in the Playhouse, which has today been designated an overflow Muster Station.

This time the voice belongs to Captain Ian Walters, who starts his well-rehearsed announcement... my mind begins to wander... I know I should concentrate, but we have done this many times before.

I bet the hairdressers have been busy, I think as I gaze along the rows of neatly coiffured heads. Light hair, dark hair, grey hair, strawberry blondes – oh yes they still do – a colourful spectrum from white to dark brown, even to jet black 'I-will-never-grow-old' coloured hair. Not a hair is out of place – what hair would dare to move under such strict control of the extra strength hair spray? After all, these hair creations have to last through to the Captain's Welcome Aboard cocktail party tomorrow evening. I mustn't forget to mention the many bald-heads that lurk between the curls. Is this what cruising does to men – strips the hair off their heads in the strong breeze that often blows across the decks? In recent years we have spent over a year afloat on various cruises from banana boats to the *QE2*, in the North and South Atlantic Oceans, Indian Ocean, Mediterranean, Adriatic, Arctic, North Sea and Baltic – oops, I nearly forgot the Nile. I glance at Himself. His head is still very well covered, so that theory is obviously wrong. There are of course plenty of men with plenty of hair, lots of ladies with longer, straighter hair, and quite a few children with naturally blonde hair to die for, but for the moment I amuse myself watching the lights bounce off the shiny bald heads.

Captain Walters is still speaking. "It is P&O policy to assemble passengers in a safe area in case of emergency..."

The woman behind me is obviously not listening to him either.

"I've only been on a small ship before," she announces to her neighbour in the next seat. "That was on the *Victoria*," she adds.

"I've not been on *Aurora* before, but I have been on *Oriana* and they are the same," he replies, enjoying a little one-upmanship! I resist the temptation to turn and tell her that he's quite wrong. They are, in fact, very different ships.

"The General Emergency Signal," the Captain ploughs on ignoring the people behind us, "is NOT the signal to abandon ship."

A slight wave of nervous laughter flits across the Playhouse from the people who are listening to his every word, and I hope that all the passengers hear the word 'not'!

"We have some very young people on board," he continues to the accompaniment of a young child's cry and gentle laughter from his audience – and a few groans, most of us grateful that we're well past it where children are concerned. "... and special life jackets are available for children under 70lbs."

Not a signal to jump overboard! Why should we want to? We are still in British waters, where it is deep, wet and probably very cold.

"In the unlikely event of having to take to the water, pinch your nose with your right hand, covering your mouth with that hand." The staff member demonstrating this procedure is standing on the stage looking slightly self-conscious.

"Place your left hand over the life jacket, hold onto the neck of the life jacket to stop it rising up..." I find myself automatically placing my right hand to my nose.

"Look down to see the space below is clear, walk forward and step off. Do Not Jump!"

Do Not Jump! Did I miss something? 76,000 tons seems very solid beneath my ample body. Would I leave it voluntarily? And after all, why do we have lifeboats? There are lots of these hanging above the Promenade Deck. Why should I want to immerse my body in the cold water of the Solent or anywhere else, for that matter?

I catch up again with the Captain whose voice over

the intercom has continued throughout the conversation behind me.

"Do not throw anything overboard and if you see anyone jump or fall overboard, throw something over the side which will float, preferably a lifebelt, and shout MAN OVERBOARD"... presumably, regardless of the sex of the person in the water.

And then it's our turn, and we're all standing up and trying them on, the life jackets. There's a general tearing of the Velcro strips as the main sections of the life jackets are eagerly ripped apart – such a satisfying noise as this tells me that this Emergency Drill is almost over. Heads are very gently put through the resulting gap – think about your new hair do – and the Velcro strips are reconnected with relief. Straps are wrapped around waists. My strap covers my bra strap, which is not where God intended my waist should be!

"There is a light," the Captain continues, and the staff member on the stage indicates the small bulb on his life jacket, "which illuminates when immersed in water..."

Let's hope we don't get to try that one out! The only water I intend to come into contact with on this cruise will be when I shower and clean my teeth at the end of another hard day's cruising.

"... and a whistle to attract attention..."

A small boy's hands escape those of his anxious mother. He grabs her whistle and blows, causing more laughter from the audience. The passengers are now getting rather bored as all of them want to get on with their holiday.

There's more ripping of the Velcro strips as the life jackets are removed – not an easy feat in the confines of the Playhouse, used for piano recitals and as a cinema.

And then it's all over and we slowly retrace our steps to our cabin where we replace the life jackets on the high shelf in the wardrobe. Hopefully they will not see the light of day again until the next occupants of this suite attend their Emergency Drill at the start of their cruise.

Now standing together on the balcony, hand in hand, Himself says: "We're listing. Definitely listing to starboard!"

I give him a withering look.

"It's because we're going round a bend – the Isle of Wight's out there!" I add, picking up the Champagne glass. There is still plenty of fizz left in the bubbles making it quite hard for me to get a meniscus – but I persevere!

A Martello Tower floats past, or at least it appears to as this large, white, lady steams steadily into the main channel and carries on her relentless course towards the Bay of Biscay. *Aurora* is so big, and sometimes it is difficult to remember that we are afloat!

"I'm just off for a lie down before dinner," Himself leaves me on the balcony where I sit for a while longer, mind in neutral, already feeling the tension in my body relax, as my stress levels plummet.

The seas are calm and the clouds are hanging high enough to allow the sun's last few rays to light the balcony. There is always plenty of traffic in this busy shipping route and my eyelids become heavy as I watch the ferries motor past and the remaining few small boats turn for home, having followed us out of Southampton.

Bing Bong! "Good evening Ladies and Gentlemen." I hear the loudspeaker in the corridor outside the cabin door burst into life again. "Dinner is being served in the Medina and Alexandria Restaurants. Do have an *amazing* evening on board *Aurora*."

The first sitting for dinner has just been announced. We still have two hours before our second sitting at 20.30. Snores filter from the bed area. The Champagne bottle is almost empty.

A black coffee is now the order of the day as I make a few last telephone calls from my mobile. They are cheaper before we leave British waters, and telephone calls made via the cabin telephone are expensive, bouncing as they do off a satellite somewhere up above, the physics of which quite escapes me.

"Just enjoying a glass of Champagne," I tell my friend Margaret.

"I thought you didn't like it. Thought it got up your nose!"

"Only when I have to pay for it," I reply with an alcohol-induced giggle.

"It's pouring down here," says Jackie.

"Great," I reply as I go into the cabin and close the balcony door to keep out the now chilly breeze. "Just what we need for the garden, but the sun's shining here!"

And my Mother says: "Did your friends make it?"

"I hope not," I laugh. "They're on board with us in September. I don't want anyone to interrupt this cruise. We need our rest."

* * * * *

Bing Bong! "Good evening Ladies and Gentlemen. Second sitting for dinner is now being served in the Alexandria and Medina Restaurants. Do have a *beautiful* evening on board *Aurora*."

Champagne consumed, and a stiff black coffee after it, somehow dinner doesn't really appeal any longer, but we must make an appearance to meet our new table companions.

We're on a round table for eight in the centre of the Alexandria Restaurant. The dress code tonight is casual – now don't worry about dress codes, as I'll explain all about them in a later chapter – for the moment stay dressed just as you are.

Casual may well be P&O's official dress code for this evening, but it's not mine or most of the other ladies on board. There will be some who take it literally and really dress down. The majority will not. We are, of course, meeting our fellow table-mates for the first time and all being well, we will spend most nights of this cruise eating dinner at the same table. If you were able to video tonight's dinner with its newly introduced table companions and compare it with the same people at the dinner which will take place on the last evening of the cruise, you would see a tremendous difference and it will be hard to recognise the people who by then will be relaxed and chatty.

'Standing on ceremony' will be the name of the game tonight. Casual we may be in name, but casual we certainly won't be in fact. Most of the men will dress down with open necked shirts and possibly a sweater, but the ladies will not. The jacket on my trouser suit will rest casually on my shoulders, but that's as casual as I'll be – only I will know that I bought it half price in the sale at my favourite boutique! Oh yes! A casual night! We shall definitely all be watching our Ps and Qs this evening.

2

F.T.C. x 2

Except we didn't... mind our Ps and Qs last night at dinner.

On reaching the lift, I pressed the call button and waited for Himself to catch me up as the lift arrived.

"Good evening," I said, to the two occupants already in the lift as we entered.

"I wonder if we'll all be quite so keen to go to dinner by the end of the cruise?" I asked them with a smile.

The lift doors were starting to close, when a lady's arm appeared as if from nowhere and the lift doors automatically swung open again. Two people rushed in. I glanced at the newcomers and vaguely thought that I'd seen them somewhere before.

Cruising gets like this – the more you cruise, the more often you see people from previous cruises.

"Good heavens – I don't believe it!" Himself's incredulous voice dragged my thoughts back to the present.

"It can't be! Jean and Terry! Where did you come from? And why didn't you tell us you were coming?"

By now we were descending steadily towards the dining room and, much to the amusement of the other couple in the lift, there was a general hugging, kissing and much rejoicing. Words tumbled out, all four of us speaking at the same time. The lift doors opened and we carried on chatting excitedly as we walked into the dining room.

So you see we didn't meet our intended new table companions last night. Instead we spent the dinner alone, the four of us, catching up on all the plotting and planning that had resulted in this 'chance' meeting – and I couldn't have cared what anyone was wearing!

We'd met Jean and Terry on our last cruise, when they were on their honeymoon – this had surprised us a little, after all, they were *only* 70 years old, but it's the sort of situation that you come across quite often on cruise ships, and before you ask, they didn't meet on a cruise. Each evening for over five weeks we shared a table on that cruise, so it was little wonder that I thought I'd seen them somewhere before! Our description of *Aurora* and this cruise to the Mediterranean had obviously tempted them, and on their return home they'd contacted our booking agents, booked a cabin, but had asked them to keep it secret, thus resulting in last night's surprise.

Throughout the afternoon they'd kept their heads down, Terry's, I suspect, under his ever-present baseball cap, and had lurked behind pot plants in an effort to avoid us, even squeezing into a corner at the back of the Playhouse for the Emergency Drill. The ship is huge, but it is amazing how often you see the same faces, and Terry, a Jack Nicholson look-alike, is hard to miss – just how many ice cream sellers do you know who look like Jack Nicholson?

* * * * *

Cruising is compelling, and it's easy to see why. Within two hours of arriving at the terminal building yesterday, we had been in our cabin, drink in hand, unpacking completed, the needle on the stress gauge already sinking fast – let's hope it will be the only thing to sink on this cruise! On a tension scale of one to ten, holiday preparations leave me around the level eight, but cruising is the only holiday I have found where level one to two is reached so quickly, and by the end of today it will be almost sub-zero.

Our first full day at sea has almost passed in a haze, as all sea days tend to do and with every hour taking us nearer to the sunshine, the temperature is noticeably warmer.

"I'm so glad you packed three sweaters," I say to Himself.

"Don't see you wearing your fleece," comes back the answer.

Already some passengers are wearing shorts and t-shirts for walking around the Promenade Deck, although those sitting and reading on the ample supply of chairs do appear to have the odd goose pimple.

By virtue of our position on the planet, a trip to the Mediterranean naturally involves a crossing of the Bay of Biscay – a so called truly dreadful experience with strong winds, horrendous waves, torrential rain and sick passengers heaving up their last meals all over the ship, which is littered with green faces and sick bags. Just make sure the wind is blowing in the right direction before you're sick over the side!

Except it isn't... a dreadful experience! Please ignore

the whole of the last paragraph and face reality, and let's lay to rest this myth about the Bay once and for all.

The ship is steaming steadily south with a light sea, the clouds dispersing as we head towards the Mediterranean, the sun is streaming onto the ship. This is by far the normal 'Bay of Biscay' experience. On the sheltered Lido Deck, the Sky Dome has been opened, and sunbathers are enjoying the sunshine, layers of clothing are being peeled off, layers of skin will no doubt follow for many unwary passengers. The sun at sea can be very deceptive. Cool breezes across the open decks often mask the effect the sun is having and it's only later when the skin starts to hurt that you realise what damage has been done. Many an unwary cruiser has spent the following days smothered in lotion, covered in cool clothing, lurking in the shade until their burnt skin has recovered.

Passengers on *Aurora* are exceptionally well catered for, regardless of what the weather forecasters throw at them. When the weather permits, the massive glass Sky Dome above Lido Deck is opened, and the Crystal Pool instantly becomes an impressive outdoor swimming pool. Should the weather turn inclement, as with today's early morning drizzle, the Sky Dome is closed, and the Crystal Pool returns to the status of an indoor pool.

Of course when crossing the Bay of Biscay, there are exceptions to these calm conditions. These are very rare, but, as with most good stories, it's the shocking crossings that make the headlines and stick in the mind. They certainly make better stories to tell back home in the pub! However, as we're in the Bay of Biscay, have little to do but relax, and before our brains become totally closed down, let's have my only bad crossing now to show you that they do occur. Before I go on, I must add that this was the only one I can remember in over a year afloat where I didn't sit in the sunshine and breathe in the wonderful fresh sea air to be found in the Bay. So pick up a sick bag, and be prepared.

That cruise on a smaller ship of approximately 30,000 tons which shall remain nameless, didn't start well at all! By anyone's standards, a Force 8-9 gale in the Channel is unpleasant and for the first time in my life, this normally brilliant sailor was seasick. Mind you, half of the rest of the passengers were horizontal too, so Himself and I were not alone.

On that occasion, we had driven to Dover in a gale and by the time we left our berth, we had been warned that it was a *little windy*, by "Hello – it's me again" – the Captain on the loudspeaker system, whose already familiar voice had reappeared following a very careful departure – the entrance to Dover harbour is not the largest in the world. We'd finished unpacking by this stage. I had managed to detach myself from the bathroom floor which had been repainted when the previous occupants left, but hadn't quite dried – and we were having a pre-dinner drink, very sensibly sitting down.

The ship was moving as we sat down to dinner, was a little more unstable as we went into the show afterwards and by the time we lay down to sleep, we were very glad indeed to be horizontal.

At 04.00 I awoke. The ship was really moving and I could hear running water.

"Don't be silly," I said to myself. "Of course you can hear running water – after all, you are at sea!"

So I lay there, trying to relax, as the ship heaved, tossed, rolled and creaked. It felt like being inside a cocktail shaker.

By 04.30 I could bear it no longer and had to check out this running water. So with a torch, in an effort to avoid waking Himself who is a bad sleeper, I climbed out of bed and immediately found the problem. We had water running down the inside of the bathroom wall, and also on the bedroom side of that wall which, as I found out by crawling around and patting the carpet in the dark, was causing an ever increasing wet patch on the floor.

I woke Himself.

There followed a mildly panicky phone call to Reception, who said they'd immediately send us a plumber.

The plumber came, but seeing our 'Do Not Disturb' notice, immediately went away again.

By 05.00 I rang again – having removed the notice. The plumber arrived, touched the stream of water and tasted it.

"Yuck," I said.

"Fresh water," he announced, I suspect to his relief as much as ours when you think of what it could have been – after all, there were cabins above us.

"Rough seas have probably fractured a pipe above. You'll have to evacuate."

No, before you jump to conclusions, we didn't grab our life jackets, but merely moved to another cabin with the help of a stream of stewards who carried our clothes – most cruise ships have a few empty cabins to cope with any problems of this nature. No one saw us go. No passengers were around. It was hardly surprising.

The next 24 hours are best glossed over – very quickly – but any description would have to involve sips of water and sick bags, clinging to furniture as we attempted trips to the bathroom, all interspersed with loud speaker announcements from "Hello – it's me again!" assuring us that there was "no danger in the situation!" I can't tell you what the sea looked like as I wasn't able to raise my head far enough to look out of the window.

"Are you alright?" Himself kept asking.

"Mmmm," I replied, less than convincingly, "and we must remember we're on holiday!"

"And it's costing a bloody fortune!" Himself added, before reaching for another sick bag.

It was all over in 24 hours of course – however at the time it did seem a very long 24 hours – and it didn't spoil the rest of what was a wonderful cruise with lots of laughter. After all, an enforced diet at the beginning of a cruise does leave plenty of space for the unavoidable food that follows.

Faced with that situation again, as soon as I heard "Hello – it's me again," warning of choppy seas – probably the only time you'll ever hear a man understate anything – I would immediately take two seasickness tablets that I now always carry on cruises, but they are obtainable from the Medical Centre on board. Thereafter, I would top them up as often as allowed on the packet until calmer seas are reached. These tablets worked well during very rough seas on the edge of a cyclone recently, and would easily cope with anything the Bay of Biscay could throw at us.

* * * * *

So here we are today, sitting on our balcony on the *Aurora*, the calm seas in the Bay of Biscay floating past, I'm reaching for a cooling drink, more suntan lotion, and trying to adjust the sun hat.

Situation quite normal for the Bay.

And now, you'll have to excuse me. The heady mixture of a delicious lunch, the sound of the waves swishing past as we continue steadily south, combined with the warmth of the sun is causing heavy eyelids. Tonight is the Captain's Welcome Aboard Cocktail party, followed by the Welcome Aboard Dinner. An hour's sleep in the late afternoon sunshine will reap benefits later this evening. Cruising can be quite exhausting and I can hear snoring from the bedroom area.

Bing Bong! "Good evening Ladies and Gentlemen. Dinner is now being served in the Alexandria and Medina Restaurants. Do have a *congenial* evening on board *Aurora*."

The first sitting passengers are being called to dinner. Most of them still feel very enthusiastic about meal times… during the cruise it will change for most of us… and I'll see you again when I've changed for dinner.

* * * * *

We stand in line, gentlemen on the left and their ladies on the right. The young female officer takes our names and announces us to the Captain who steps forward to shake our hands.

"Welcome aboard," he says with a beaming smile, despite the fact that we are towards the end of what has been a long queue of passengers. He seems genuinely pleased that we are on board his ship and has the knack of making everyone feel special. Captain Walters on my right and Himself on my left, we pause in mid-sentence and smile whilst the second official photograph is taken, before moving forward to accept a drink from a gloved waiter. It would not be a great idea to refuse *this* photograph – you don't want to be put ashore at the next port, do you? Again, there is no obligation to buy this or any other photograph that will be taken of you during the cruise. Most new cruisers appear to buy most photographs; us old hands become somewhat more selective. After all, just how many photographs do I want of the two of us – although it does of course chart the expansion of my waistline, if I look back to the photographs from our early cruises! (Please notice the nautical term 'chart' – well, where did you think it came from?)

Tonight is Formal – this means a Tuxedo and black tie or dark suit for gentlemen, evening gown or cocktail dress for the ladies. The room is already almost full of handsome men and attractive ladies, with not a hair out of place of course. Most of the ladies are wearing floor length gowns, skirts or trousers... if the sea does become choppy these are very useful fashion assets, in that flat shoes can be worn without causing comment, thus increasing stability. Tonight I catch sight of plenty of stiletto heels, and the floor is not moving, although of course it may do for some later in the evening.

Can these be the same crumpled, cross and harassed people whom I saw sitting in rows in the terminal building just over 24 hours ago? Gone are the weary faces and stooped shoulders. The air is filled with perfume and after-shave, the babble of excited chatter fills my ears, a gentle chuckle on my left is knocked flat by a full-blown belly laugh on my right. Stress factors have already sunk below zero. This shipload of passengers is on holiday and each person is determined to enjoy every moment on board.

Everywhere passengers are chatting animatedly with new friends, with members of the crew, young and old, waiters are weaving their way between groups offering interesting canapés and replenishing empty drinks. I spy a young officer standing alone with a lady who turns out to be his wife and for the next few minutes I immerse myself happily learning about the training programme of a Third Engineer and what life is like for his wife. She looks incredibly young and is enjoying a fortnight on board along with their two young children, having travelled down from their home in Edinburgh. The facilities on board for very young children are exceptionally good and this fortnight will indeed be a holiday for her.

We are now joined by the Second Engineer who has Gadget *in tow* – another nautical term! He is a very new graduate training to be an engineer.

"Why do you call him Gadget?" I ask.

"Because he's handy for little jobs!" comes the witty reply, causing laughter all round, and the young Gadget looks a little self conscious at being the centre of attention, but equally delighted to have a job which he plainly adores. I'm sure it won't be long before he's making that joke himself about another new recruit.

The party atmosphere continues until we are called to order by the Cruise Director. He's the guy who organises all the activities and entertainments on board. He never appears to be flustered, always has a smile and has a very attractive pair of hairy knees! I grin as I remember the evening on a previous cruise when the passengers in the theatre were made aware of this fact.

The Captain steps forward and thanks us for coming. How could we refuse? He tells us that the early morning's drizzle was the fault of the Officer he had left in charge on the Bridge (control room of the ship) and takes full credit for the wonderful sunshine this afternoon, which, of course, resulted from his intervention.

"However," he continues, "my Officers are so busy steering the ship." – He makes no mention of the computer controlled satellite guided systems on his state of the art Bridge, and we are all left thinking of a Captain Long John Silver look alike, manfully turning a giant steering wheel. Reality couldn't be further from that vision.

"If we look after the ship," he continues, "can we leave you passengers to take care of the weather?"

When the laughter subsides, he makes a few more nautical comments before wishing us all a delicious dinner and an enjoyable evening on board Aurora.

Bing Bong! "Good evening Ladies and Gentlemen. Dinner is now being served in the Alexandria and Medina Restaurants. Do have a *delectable* evening on board *Aurora*."

Tonight we have indeed met our new table companions. The four of us have joined a table hosted by the Senior First Officer, and we have two very unusual passengers at the table with us. They are 'virgin cruisers', or 'First Time Cruisers', and will henceforth be known as Mr and Mrs F.T.C. They are indeed rare items and if this were stamp collecting, they'd most certainly be Penny Blacks.

"We can't believe we've reached this age and never cruised before," laughs Mrs F.T.C., a retired Army doctor in her early 60s.

"And do you like it so far?" I ask, knowing already what the answer will be. You can tell it from their faces.

"We're hooked already," Mr F.T.C. says, laughing at his use of a pseudo nautical term.

"I couldn't have believed that we'd feel so relaxed in such a short time," he continues.

"It makes air travel seem very unappealing," adds his wife.

For the first time since we sat down, silence reigns around the table as we study the menu :

Asparagus spears wrapped in
Filo Pastry with a herb butter sauce
❖

Crab and Sweetcorn Soup
❖

Pink Champagne Sorbet
❖

Rock Lobster Tail a L'Americaine served with
Braised vegetable rice and shellfish oil
❖

Hot Chocolate Soufflé with Tia Maria Sauce
❖

Coffee and assorted chocolate Truffles
❖

Not bad for a quick snack? That's not the full menu of course, but merely what I chose. With the exception of the soup, each course has a minimum of three choices, on top of which there is a special menu for diabetics and also one for vegetarians. In fact almost any dietary requirements can be catered for, provided plenty of notice is given to the kitchen, or galley, now that we are on board a ship.

The stiffness of the first few minutes disappears as we eat our way through the dishes on the menu and get to know our new companions.

"Chichester?" I exclaim to Mr and Mrs F.T.C. who have just announced where they live.

"I don't believe it! We come from Haslemere, but I quite often pop down to Chichester."

Here follows a discussion about the merits of the shops and boutiques in Chichester, which needn't be related!

"South Derbyshire," announces Neil Turnbull, the Senior First Officer, a delightful guy whose wife is expecting their first baby in July. He's due home a week before, in time for the birth, but I don't have the heart to tell him our son arrived ten days early!

His home is about five miles from my oldest friends and both he and they frequent the same restaurant in Melbourne. The longer I cruise, the more I realise how small this world really is, although I do begin to query that comment on an Atlantic crossing!

The conversation flows non-stop, butterfly-ing into and out of subjects smoothly and only stops when we realise that we are the last table occupied in the large dining room, a sin we are to commit many times in the coming days.

"A quick night cap in the Crow's Nest?" asks Terry, but it takes us a while to find this bar on Deck 13, which is at the front of the ship. *Aurora* is large, 886 feet long (270 metres), and when you're inside and can't see the sea, it is very difficult to work out which way is FRONT!

3

LOST HOURS – CLOCKWISE & ANTICLOCKWISE!

We lost an hour! You gain some, you lose some, and last night we definitely lost.

Having found the Crow's Nest, eventually, and how many times have we been on this ship, which only goes to show you just how big she really is – we chatted until bedtime. Only it wasn't bedtime. In reality it was one hour later. Now when you're in your twenties, thirties or even forties this really doesn't matter, but when you get to our age, it makes quite a huge difference to life the following morning.

When travelling any distance from the UK you pass into different time zones – a fairly painless experience if you're going a short way or even if you are lucky enough to be gaining an hour. However, if like us last night you had it taken away, stealthily whilst you slept, your early morning tea will arrive whilst you are still dreaming of pirates, or pilates. Just as I was about to walk the plank, the Butler's voice interrupted the proceedings and pulled me back from unavoidable disaster. Disaster? Oh I don't know! He was a very handsome pirate!

"Good morning," he chirped, far too cheerfully, the Butler not the pirate. Could he be thinking of his trip home to see his parents? He flies from Heathrow to Mumbai (that's Bombay if you've not been updated) the day we return home to Southampton. The end of our holiday will be the beginning of his, although he'll not be able to guarantee good weather as he returns to India in time for the monsoon.

Satya has been working on board for six months – seven days a week, every day on every cruise – without a single day off! Can you imagine what that must feel like? To him Southampton is just another day in port, with the added work of having to get organised for the next cruise and introduce himself to his new passengers.

"Good afternoon Sir, Madam. My name is Satya and I'm your Butler."

I can remember the first time we met him, each a little unsure of the other, wondering whether we would 'click', whether we'd be on a strictly professional footing, or whether we'd get to know each other.

He's the youngest of six children, the other five have professional jobs in India – and it's not hard to imagine the joy his return home will bring, and he'll be there for three or four months.

"I enjoyed messing about in school," he once told me with a grin. "I'm the black sheep of the family! I'll do this for a while and then maybe do some studying."

He was recently offered promotion on the ship but turned it down, preferring to have close contact with his passengers.

He pulls back the curtain in the suite. I put an arm across my eyes as the room fills with bright light.

"It's a lovely day," he bounces, the clatter of teacups echoing his exuberance.

"We'll take your word for it, Satya," I grunt.

The temptation to turn over is great and I succumb. He's back half an hour later with our breakfast tray.

"I've got some lovely mango this morning," he cheerfully chants as he lays out our cereals and fruit, composing his own melody with the cutlery.

"Thank you Satya," I grunt again.

"It's going to be a really beautiful day," he won't give in.

"I'm so glad," I grunt with feeling.

"What are you going to do today?"

"Sleep!" I can't put it more plainly.

"Well, have a nice day Madam," he exits cheerfully to move on to his next breakfast tray, and no doubt spread a little more joy along the corridor.

"Just another few moments," I think as I bury my head in the pillow.

But no! There's a noise from the bathroom. I warily open one eye and pat the bed beside me. It's empty, and with all the agility of an arthritic snail, I slowly slither to my feet. Another fun-filled day on the good ship *Aurora* has begun.

Not only have we had an hour stolen, we now have to move swiftly into action, or one meal will run into another on sea days. Life on board for some revolves around meal times and we have to work hard to eat breakfast and lunch before enjoying another delicious meal this evening – and there are some who want to fit in afternoon tea as well.

Every cloud has a silver lining, unless of course it's in

a tropical storm, and that which has been stolen from us will be returned to us on our way home. However, this silver lining will be somewhat tarnished, as an extra hour encourages a late night enjoying the on board entertainment. It's almost like an invitation to party. How many times have I heard the comment, "Let's have another drink. We have an extra hour tonight!"

On journeys across the Atlantic these time changes can be a major problem. It's wonderful going west when you gain an hour several nights in succession, but coming home and travelling east it can be very tiring. On these crossings, P&O cleverly minimises the effect by moving the clock forwards at lunchtime, rather than in the middle of the night. On these days you dare not breakfast late, or your last mouthful of scrambled egg will be chased by an army of chips, and swiftly followed by apple crumble. You may think it's midday, your stomach may think it's midday, but in the blink of an eye the daily announcement from the Bridge at noon says, "Ship's time has become 13.00," and we must remember that afternoon tea starts at 16.30. Anyone on early dinner at 18.30 barely has time to leave the restaurant.

Some passengers are upset because the hour lost reduces the time that lunch is actually available! They forget the extra drinking time they gained on the journey west. It is hardly surprising that westbound crossings of the Atlantic become one long party night!

Time changes both ways also cause logistical problems. No matter how many times we are told, passengers often forget. A note on the table at dinner advising of the time change is of course forgotten after a couple of nightcaps and more than one passenger has found breakfast the following morning has finished, when he thinks he's just arrived in time. Never mind –

do not worry about him too much – he doesn't have long to wait for lunch, or he could visit the ever-open Café Bordeaux, or even call for room service. It is quite unheard of for a passenger to die from starvation.

And here we'll expand, as many waistlines are already doing, and talk about an unfortunate subject – I'll try and say it gently – flab! Pounds of the stuff – or, if you prefer it, kilos, although the figures on the scales would appear to make you even heavier, so I'll stick to pounds, and I'll hold in my stomach whilst I do it.

We all have it, in varying quantities – well most of us do – and if you're at all squeamish about the subject, move swiftly over the next few paragraphs...

Have you ever thought how strong your ankles are? Progress that further – ponder on the complexities of your knee joints, and the pressure exerted on your hips. From my younger days I remember stiletto heels and the weight on their tiny tips being the equivalent to the weight of an elephant standing on a mint – or was it a fox? Maybe I have the equation wrong, but I am sure you get the meaning. I think I may even still have a pair of those opaque plastic covers for stiletto heels, which we used to wear to protect unsuspecting polished floors and carpets. As teenagers we carried them in our handbags, ready for instant use – a little different to the contents of some teenagers' handbags these days... and I have never seen stiletto heel covers on sale in public lavatories!

But back to the ankles! All this weight is contained in seemingly elastic bodies, now intent on increasing their size. On most people, the ankles and wrists are the narrowest parts of the body. Have you noticed how fat ladies often have very slim ankles, quite out of proportion with the rest of their overweight bodies? No matter how you try, it does seem almost impossible to put weight on around your ankles unless, of course, you have a medical problem. I normally cannot speak for men. They are extremely lucky because their extremities are usually covered by trousers. However, on my last cruise, I spent a lot of time looking down, supposedly examining the deck timbers, but in truth checking on male ankles as they walked past – imagine how demure I must have seemed! On the whole, the same statement would appear to apply to men also as few overweight ankles made it into my census.

OK. So what do we do on board ship?

Well, we eat – not a slimming occupation, as undressed salads appear to be indecent and therefore not very tempting, although, of course, they are always on offer. There is seldom a long queue at the salad counter.

We drink – you're hardly likely to swallow water to the exclusion of all other liquids throughout the holiday, although it would certainly be more beneficial in warmer climates.

We watch the sea with minds in neutral, and this is seldom energetic!

We read our books, slightly more energetic – think about the effort involved turning the pages.

We talk a lot, but sore jaws do not make for slim bodies.

We sleep, and depending on how long the goodnight kiss stage lasts, this may or may not consume a few calories!

Half an hour in the gym, line dancing, deck games and walking in ever decreasing circles around the deck may all mitigate the effects of the dining room, but it is only the very determined and most careful of eaters who disembark the same weight they were on embarkation day.

I shall not!

I've heard it said that it is possible whilst on a cruise to put weight on at the rate of a pound a day – and indeed some people on board will do just that, and more. We are on this cruise for fourteen days. I was not skinny to start with and, as my maths is appalling, I'll leave you to do the arithmetic. Please do not send me your answers – my shrinking clothes tell their own sad story.

Partly, I think the sea air is to blame as it obviously causes shrinkage. However, I also blame elastic and whoever invented it should be shot. True, without it our knickers would fall down, but doubtless some other way of keeping these garments in place would by now have been found. It is amazing how a tight waistband concentrates the mind at mealtimes, and how the discomfort and reduced space for lungs to expand stops even the most delicious looking chocolate cake from being tempting.

How many of us sigh with relief when a new outfit is found to have an elastic waist? "Perfect for a holiday," we say – whether land-based or afloat.

And before the men presume to gloat, the following is for you!

There are indeed differences between the sexes – apologies for using that word – it must be the effects of the sun, now that we're well past the Bay of Biscay. The differences are well known, and appreciated. But there is one major difference that as a female I find very sad. It is where we human beings carry our fat.

Take yesterday afternoon – Cocktail of the Day in hand... (You can find details of these drinks in *Aurora*

Today. This also gives all the shipboard information and times of Today's Events and is delivered to your cabin late the evening before.)... a Sea Breeze Cooler – a mixture of gin, apricot brandy, lemon juice, lots of crisp crackling ice, soda water and a dash of grenadine. I was looking down from a quarterdeck, mind in neutral, watching the sea slosh past, the sun was blazing down on several bodies fast turning mahogany. It was then I caught sight of him, the back of a bronzed Adonis. No doubt his wonderful tan was just getting topped up as he must have brought most of it on board with him – we haven't been away from Southampton long enough for him to be that colour. A heavy gold chain hung around his neck, glinting in the sunshine as he stood, hands on the rail, gazing out to sea.

He was tallish with a good head of hair, a few damp curls nestling into the nape of his neck. I allowed my eyes to follow his broad shoulders and wander down his muscular back, pausing at his very nice little bottom. He was wearing an attractive pair of swimming trunks – you know, the old fashioned, multi-coloured, stretchy variety that leave very little to the imagination, so I let my mind wander, eventually taking in his absolutely *wonderful* pair of legs.

I ran my hand through my hair as sexy thoughts began to trickle into my head. I pictured his bronzed hands applying sun tan lotion to my back, my shoulders, my arms and further... I could almost feel his hands, gentle but persuading, increasingly covering my body with Factor 20, the hot sun beating down, heating my blood, increasing my heart rate. Parts of me stirred. Parts of me yearned. Desire, anticipation, expectation!

And then he broke the spell.

He turned sideways. Was this man really a woman

about to give birth? He was, to put it bluntly, fat. F.A.T. Fat. It cannot be put more kindly for he was truly gynormous. A good profile, but he was still fat. And where were his swim shorts? To my amazement they had disappeared. Somewhere under the over-hang of his eight and a half month pseudo-pregnancy, they had totally disappeared, along with all my desire. Splash! Just as though a bucket of ice-cold water had been poured over me. All my desire and anticipation vanished in that instant. Suddenly I was left with no expectations whatsoever.

See what I mean? Men are indeed lucky. I have no doubt at all that were I to meet this guy on the stairs and if he were in evening dress, I would again be interested. His flab would be hidden, tucked neatly into his shirt, firmly held in place by a strong belt, or maybe assisted by a stout pair of braces, a smart dinner jacket disguising his excessive weight. Men are able to wear their flab above their belts – regrettably we ladies are not.

Picture now a lady in his place. Her excess weight would be obvious immediately, and show from all directions. From the back she would look large, her hips would bulge, her waist would be non-existent, and her arms would be baggy and saggy. From the side her chins would cascade onto her chest, and her boobs and tum would meet. The first apparent separation in the fat would be at her knees and yes, only her ankles and possibly her wrists would be slim. In her evening dress, still she would not be able to disguise it. She would resemble a battleship in full sail, albeit, should she possess a pretty face, an attractive battleship.

And what about attitudes? It's OK for a man to possess a beer gut! Indeed, it can even be something to be proud of. He's 'one of the guys, a great chap, a good sport, he buys his rounds'. Try thinking of one compliment to say about a fat lady!

And this is why I would shoot the inventor of elastic. By the time elastic waists will stretch no more, the damage is well and truly done. The need to go up a whole dress size can be achieved before the point of no further stretch is reached. At that stage it is just so much easier to visit your favourite dress shop and exclaim: "Oh perfect, an elastic waist! How wonderful! It'll be brilliant for the next cruise!" And the whole process starts again.

Is there an answer to the problem? Yes indeed I believe there is. It's a diet before your holiday – a pre-cruise diet. On my last cruise I met a man who did just that, and then told me he'd lost two *whole* pounds before the holiday! I didn't have the heart to tell him that two pounds wouldn't last me more than a couple of days. And then, just to make sure he avoided problems, he had actually visited his tailor and asked him to let out his trousers, by a *whole* inch! Now that's what I call belt and braces! Lunch for him most days appeared to be something a caterpillar had overlooked... and certainly there was no alcohol in sight. Most passengers are unable to be quite so disciplined.

Failing that, there is only one answer – and I have to confess that I am a little surprised that the cruise companies haven't already thought of this one – a tax on fat!

If all cruise ship operators charged a fat tax per pound of extra weight gained during a holiday, allowing a small amount of leeway, people would be careful – or maybe they'd just cheat! Which of you have been to the initial weigh-in at a Slimming Club wearing the heaviest pair of shoes you possess, only to wear sandals next week? Need I say more?

So be warned – cruising is not a slimming occupation. And not only that, losing an hour last night has reduced the time my body has had to digest dinner. I wonder to whom I should address my letter of complaint!

Of course I paint the worst possible picture. There are plenty of slim people on board – indeed I used to be one myself! – but I don't want the skinny ones amongst you to start thinking that cruising is not for you. Every coin has two sides, and the second side of *Aurora* is up and *running* at this moment.

Everywhere there is plenty of activity, and not only in the gym. Do you realise that 3.2 circuits of Promenade Deck equates to a distance of one mile? However, as the notice on the wall of Promenade Deck carries on to say, "Jogging and Exercise Walking is prohibited between 11:00pm and 7:30am", although I can't imagine why anyone should want to at that time of the morning.

Walking around the deck is a popular occupation. I'm an anti-clockwise person myself. I can't explain why, but I *never* walk clockwise around a ship. What will you be? Some people only walk in a clockwise direction as I start to recognise the same faces each day going around the Promenade Deck, and nearly always we smile at each other. After the first day the occasional person speaks as they go past, but by virtue of the speed each of us is travelling, only a couple of words are exchanged before we pass again on the other side of the ship. As you can imagine, it does take some time to amass a whole sentence! However, passing acquaintances are often seen inside the ship and more lengthy conversations can follow.

There are also the competitors of the world who have to walk faster than anyone else on board. I try to maintain a constant speed; clearly they do not. Beads of perspiration break out as they push themselves harder and harder, determined to gain a few feet before we pass each other on the starboard side. By the port side crossover, they're looking quite smug as they're obviously gaining on me, and when they can't find me on the next starboard side crossing because I've nipped inside for a large plate of afternoon tea, they're dreadfully disappointed and immediately find someone else to race!

Some cruise lines reward you for taking part in activities by giving vouchers for each half hour of exercise. These can be collected for *valuable* prizes at the end of the cruise, and fierce competition prevails. I hated competitions at school and regret I haven't improved since, so I am more than willing to donate any vouchers I have been careless enough to collect to any needy soul. These can be exchanged for such magnificent prizes as key rings and bookmarks! – but it's the taking part that's important!

If you are travelling by yourself you could have joined "Walk a Mile" with Shaun at 08.00 this morning – no dressing gowns will be allowed! This is an easy way to meet fellow passengers – you all walk in the same direction of course – as is the Morning Coffee and Travelling Alone Get Together at 10.30. There really is no need ever to feel alone on board ship, unless of course you choose to.

The gym on board is full of ghastly looking equipment of torture, apart from the treadmills that I recognise. Machines that will put muscles on muscles, cycles where you can pedal away for dear life all morning and never move an inch, and occasionally when I've been standing there, vainly trying to work out how to start my treadmill, the exercise floor has swarmed with bodies, male and female, in sexy outfits flinging arms this way and legs that way, in time to loud music with a strong beat – all under the watchful eyes of a *sympathetic* instructor!

Aurora has three swimming pools and four Jacuzzis, golf simulator and nets, and sports court. Each day *Aurora Today* advertises Tennis, Cricket, Shuffleboard, and Deck Quoits. Dancing classes, where today you can learn to do the Tango, Line dancing, Table Tennis and Aerobics classes.

For those who prefer mental agility there are activities such as Bridge, Whist, Computer Lessons, the Individual Quiz and after dinner the Syndicate Quiz. Port enhancement talks on each of the ports *Aurora* will visit this cruise, lectures, films and recitals. The list seems endless and there is no excuse to feel bored. It is much more likely that at the end of each day there'll be shouts of: "I missed that talk on Reflexology this morning!" Days on board ship are never long enough. And, before we leave the exercise subject, don't ever think that deck quoits and shuffleboard are sissy games played by feeble females and cowardly, effeminate males – nothing could be further from the truth! You have been warned.

It's been a busy day. Cake Decorating Demonstration, a morning Classical Music Concert, a two-litre alcoholic lunch in the Café Bordeaux, two miles walking around the Promenade deck and a Maritime Lecture – and I didn't have time to enjoy any afternoon tea.

Bing Bong! "Good evening Ladies and Gentlemen. Dinner is now being served in the Alexandria and Medina Restaurants. Do have a *fabulous* evening on board *Aurora*."

And yes, before you ask, you did miss out on his earlier announcement when he wished everyone an "*enjoyable*" evening – I thought I'd leave you to sleep through it, and try to gather energy for tonight's entertainments – another classical concert and a show in the Curzon Theatre. You have to be energetic to keep up with the pace here on board *Aurora*.

4

GOLD AND ROCKS

Today is Wednesday, and I only know that because I've cheated and looked at *Aurora Today*. Underneath a picture of *Aurora* I see there's a Double Bill Cabaret in the Curzon Theatre tonight – a singer and an illusionist, although in my day they were called conjurers – and a Sailaway Party on Deck at 12.30pm.

Already, as they always have a habit of doing on board ship, one day is blending into another seamlessly.

"Did we have lunch in the restaurant yesterday, or was that the day before?"

"What day is it – Tuesday or Wednesday?"

"When do we arrive at…?"

"Is it a sea day today?"

Passengers are a confused crowd who have already been lulled into a relaxed stupor, punctuated by fresh air and food and the occasional alcoholic beverage – and we've only been at sea two days… or is it three?

But today must be Wednesday, for not only does the Ship's Newspaper giving us yesterday's UK news state so, but out there, as I look from our balcony, is a very large rock. We are in Gibraltar, and because it's British, we can still use the dear old Pound.

Great excitement! This is *your* first port of call!

As you will come to realise, there are two kinds of port. The first, like today, where the ship is tied up alongside the quay, and the second where she lays at anchor off shore, either because the harbour is just too small to take a large ship like *Aurora*, or because the sea is too shallow. The thought of *Aurora* being stuck on a sandbank or holed by a rock just doesn't bear thinking about. Obviously being tied up along side is much easier for us passengers who can come and go as we please, just showing our cruise card as we leave the ship, and again when we return.

When at anchor, the ship's lifeboats are used as tenders to ferry passengers from the ship to the shore and back again. There are up to 1,870 passengers on board, and the logistics of getting most of these to the shore at a tender port are very complicated.

To start with, the lifeboats have to be lowered into the water – at least this ensures that their mechanisms are regularly checked in case, in the unlikely event of an emergency, they are needed at sea – and then they are positioned at the side of *Aurora* where a platform at the side of the ship has been opened, capable of accommodating two lifeboats at a time. Plenty of strong sailors are on hand to ensure safe transfer from the ship to tender and vice versa.

Rather than all 1,870 passengers trying to get onto the very first lifeboat – and human nature being what it is, we would *all* like to be on that *first* tender – P&O and other cruise lines have devised a system whereby you collect a numbered ticket and then sit quietly in the theatre until the group containing your number is called. I never cease to marvel at the speed and efficiency of this procedure, and rarely is there a long wait in the theatre, normally just time to digest breakfast and certainly not long enough to catch up on last night's sleep!

Wheelchair bound? Not a problem! P&O will ensure that most disabled passengers will be able to experience the delights of whatever port we are visiting. The only exception may be the state of the landing stage at the shore side. That has prevented the landing of wheelchair passengers on occasions, but this is indeed rare.

At the end of the day in a 'tender port' there is the added excitement of watching the lifeboats being brought back on board, which is a delicate operation especially in choppy seas. Long time cruisers are an experienced bunch and consider that we know at least as much as the Captain, and possibly even more! Often a loud cheer will go up from the balconies where the passengers have been watching the operation, when the incredibly young looking officer driving the tender has positioned it in such a way that the two crewmen have been able to connect with the steel cables and large hooks, and the lifeboat is winched back on board *Aurora*. This is often followed by Captain Walter's announcement that he has all his ducklings back on board, accompanied to more cheering from his passengers. Passengers and crew do not take long to become one happy family, and the more you cruise, the more nautically minded you become.

But back to today, where we are firmly tied up at the quayside. Breakfast was early, the sun is shining, and by 09.00 we are on dry land. The mini bus drivers of Gibraltar are in lines waiting to take us the short distance from the quay to the start of the shopping street. Please each of you have an English Pound coin ready to pay for your seat. If you prefer to walk, it's only a short distance, but can seem a lot longer on the return journey, especially if your hands are full with goodies!

Now Gibraltar means different things to different people. To the majority, most of whom have been here innumerable times before, it's a chance to increase the gross weight of the ship by several tons of cheap, duty free alcohol, cigarettes and perfume, all of which are considerably cheaper here than in the UK. P&O's bar profits will take a dip for a few days until these supplies have been exhausted. But to others it's a chance to sample the history of a cosmopolitan outpost of Great Britain, where Sterling is still acceptable.

There is plenty to see in Gibraltar, especially on your first visit, and most of it is within walking distance, but remember the Rock is steep and it will be easier to take a local taxi. Because we invariably only stay half a day, there may possibly be enough to interest you on a second visit, but after that, you'll probably join the bulk of the passengers now strolling along Main Street.

A first visit to the Rock would not be complete without a trip to the caves and tunnels once used as barracks, hospitals and kitchens. A trip in the Cable Car to the top of the Rock should be considered, as on a clear day this gives fantastic views of Gibraltar, the Mediterranean, the Straits of Gibraltar and even of North Africa. The fee for the Cable Car includes entry to the Apes Den, and St. Michael's Cave, where concerts are performed.

Mention Gibraltar and most people think of the apes, but they are in fact monkeys, a tailless species called Barbary Macaques and found wild in Morocco and Algeria. Exciting stories of underground tunnels linking Gibraltar with North Africa abound, but the more likely method of their transportation across the 14 kilometres from the African coast was by boat. Soft and cuddly with cute faces, tame they may appear, but remember they are wild animals and very partial to handbags and cameras, preferably the more expensive ones. If you upset them, they can and will bite. They are under the control of the Government and the Army supplies them with food, so any of them that try to convince you that they are hungry, are probably telling porky pies. On our first visit to Gibraltar, we found their favourite food was sweets, which they're not allowed, and they seemed to enjoy dry, uncooked pasta – obviously being confined to the Rock has affected their brains! Each birth and death is registered and apparently they all have a name – this seems to be a lot of fuss to go to for a bunch of monkeys, but possibly at the back of their minds, the government officials remember the legend that states Gibraltar will cease to be British if the monkeys leave the Rock.

The slopes of the Rock, which rise to 419 metres, are also the home to rabbits and would you believe it, porcupines and rattlesnakes, although thankfully I've not come across either of those. You certainly don't see them slithering along Main Street.

It's great for bird watchers – the feathered variety now we're off the ship, please – as twice a year in spring and autumn, birds migrating to and from North Africa cross the Straits and rest in Gibraltar before carrying on their journeys. Eucalyptus, pine and olive trees, originally planted to prevent land erosion, grow on the upper slopes, and on the lower ones you'll find a profusion of brooms, bougainvillaea, honeysuckle, lavender and jasmine – always assuming you get past the shopkeepers!

Gibraltar is where Nelson's body was brought ashore after the Battle of Trafalgar, so you'll not be surprised to find several museums and statues. There is, in fact, plenty to keep any man in your company occupied whilst you concentrate on the matter in hand!

To me Gibraltar is where I buy my earrings, but should I really confess that, when he saw me, a delightful Indian guy unlocked his shop where he was preparing for opening time at 10.00 and came out and greeted me like a long lost friend?

"I see you're wearing the earrings you bought last visit," he beamed as he shook my hand.

"Are you coming to see me?" his perfect Omo-white teeth echoed the sparkle in his deep brown eyes, no doubt the thought of the sound of the cash register ringing in his ears. "Come and meet my wife. She'll be here shortly."

"So you got married since our last visit," I was genuinely pleased to see him. He's one of those tall, dark, handsome guys whom I'd first met as a trainee in his parent's jewellery shop, and he now has an equally gorgeous wife. By the look of her lack of waist, he's found a certain way of ensuring the continuation of the family business.

Did I really need another pair of earrings? Well, it would have been churlish to refuse.

We are still smiling as we leave the shop, having shaken hands with Mother, Son and new production member of the family team. And where do you think he and his bride spent their honeymoon? On a cruise of course!

Passengers and crew mingle happily along the main

shopping street. I catch sight of the Third Engineer and his wife from Edinburgh with their two small boys, all hungrily tucking into huge plates piled high with eggs, sausages, baked beans and chips.

"Just come off duty," he says, as my eyes widen at the size of the portions.

Notices in the shop windows read 'Special discounts for *Aurora* passengers'. They do, of course, have a pile of these notices, and are prepared for every cruise ship which ventures through the Straits of Gibraltar. Last time we visited, we were greeted with 'Gibraltar welcomes *Braemar* passengers', one of Fred. Olsen's ships.

Today we arrived at 08.00 and will leave at 13.00. Because of the political implications, trips from here across the border into Spain are very difficult with inevitable delays, and visits to Gibraltar do often last for only five hours. As you lose approximately half an hour at each end of the visit for port clearance on arrival and ship's departure procedures as you sail, this leaves a maximum of four hours to explore the area, or to remind your credit card company that you are still alive.

Of course, cruises are a temporary holiday for your credit card in that no cash, cheques or cards are used whilst on board – except in the casino, Bingo, buying postage stamps and tipping, of which more later. Every passenger is issued with a card giving name and cabin number. This records you leaving and returning to the ship when in port, and it is this that is used to pay for extras – purchases in the shops, treatments in the Beauty Salon, laundry, alcohol, photographs etc. Every item is charged via the ship's card to your personal account and it is the total of this account that is eventually debited to your credit card at the completion of the voyage.

Your card will have enjoyed a short holiday and if

you've judged the timing right, the damage you inflicted on your ship's account at 02.00 when you cried "Drinks all round!" will not be paid for until probably next month, and may well be closely followed by a deposit for the next cruise. One cruise does tend to be followed by another!

But we must hurry back on board as the ship is now preparing to leave.

"All our departure checks have been completed and *Aurora* is ready to depart for sea," the Captain's voice floats across the open decks.

We've misjudged it. A quick snack lunch and then the departure party on the open deck, we said... but as things do on board ship, it turned into a rather longer lunch than expected.

We were half way through our incredibly healthy salad when Ivy and Ethel joined our table in the Orangery, the self-service buffet on Deck 12. We thought we had chosen the Orangery for its speed. In the event our discussion over the differences and merits of the cruise ships in P&O's fleet saw Gibraltar disappearing rapidly into the haze.

Ivy and Ethel were two 'mature' ladies from Lancashire, whose laughter and wrinkles will linger in our memories.

"*Aurora* is too big," said Ivy.

"We liked *Victoria*," said Ethel.

They nodded together.

"You could spend a whole cruise alone on here," said Ivy.

More nodding.

"I'm on a diet today," said Ethel, biting into her cream filled apple turnover. "I'm only having a light lunch," she added as she licked the cream off her fingers. "I suppose I should have got a knife and cut it."

"Do as you'd do at home, lass, and eat it," countered Ivy.

"I do like these paper napkins – better than them material ones – don't you?" Ethel asked, looking at me.

Bemused by the blob of cream as it moved up and down on her top lip, I missed the question and didn't answer. She probably thought I was deaf.

* * * * *

"We'll have a quiet afternoon," Himself decrees.

"We have to be organised early this evening. We have an invitation to another cocktail party," I reply, reaching for the Factor 20.

The sea is so flat it resembles a millpond. So often the early afternoon seas become calm and peaceful, almost mirroring the attitude of passengers on board. The odd piece of rubbish floats past to break the monotony, a turtle sunbathing on the surface until it becomes aware of *Aurora* gently passing and slips below for safety – at least I think it was a turtle. What else resembles a meat pie with a leg at each corner and has a long, wrinkled neck? Two birds, like huge brown seagulls, are half-heartedly fishing for lunch and a shoal of tiny fish is playing around a polythene bag discarded by some careless person somewhere in the world. It's hardly Wild Life on One, but it is life all the same. Not a cloud in the sky, the hot sun seems to make even the water dozy in the post lunch hour of rest. We are here on the balcony laying on our sun beds in the shade, soaking up the peace and tranquillity; the gentle slop, slop, slop of the bow wave being the only sound to break the silence.

A sudden leap into activity and a grab for the binoculars as Himself spots a school of dolphins frolicking in the warm afternoon sun – eight or ten of them splashing around, quite oblivious to us until the noise of our engines reaches them and they disappear, only to re-emerge behind the ship to continue their play in our wake when we are safely past. And then he spots a huge fish – maybe a small whale. It's about half a mile off the starboard side, the silver of his body shining in the sun as it breaks the surface – he's gently cruising along. No fin, so it's not a shark, but whatever it is, it is a large sea creature. And now he too has gone.

Excitement over and back to our peaceful cruise across the silky waters, eyelids becoming heavy, breathing becoming slower, snoring becoming louder.

It doesn't look much on a map, but the Mediterranean is large. We've been sailing all afternoon and all we've seen is one small sailing boat. Mind you, the port side of the ship might have been like Clapham Junction, but peace reigns supreme on this side.

Bing Bong! "Good evening Ladies and Gentlemen. Dinner is now being served in the Alexandria and Medina Restaurants. Do have a *gorgeous* evening on board *Aurora*."

That interrupts Himself in mid-snore.

"Where did the afternoon go?" he mutters as he looks at his watch.

"We'll have to hurry if we're to make drinks at 8 o'clock," I reply, offering him one of our canapés, king prawns with a spicy dip today.

"Gin and tonic?" he asks.

"No thanks, but I'd love a cuppa."

Tonight is the POSH Club cocktail party. If this is your first cruise, then regrettably you won't be able to join us, but when you return to Southampton, do make sure you join in time for your next cruise. POSH, as many of us know, stands for Port Out and Starboard Home, from the days before air conditioning, when the only way to get a cool cabin on the way to India was on the Port side of the ship. Nowadays, of course, there is no need for such careful choice of cabins, although on a crossing of the Atlantic, it can get pretty gloomy if you're always on the shady side of the ship.

The POSH Club is what P&O has named its loyalty club for passengers and to join you must have been on a previous P&O cruise within the past ten years. Other cruise companies have their loyalty clubs, and they are conducted in similar ways. P&O say it is an exclusive club, but looking at the crush tonight, you might be forgiven for thinking otherwise. For a small fee you gain membership entitling you to a newsletter four times a year, and early notification of next year's cruise programme, along with special discounts on selected cruises at short notice. Add to this discounts in the on-board shops and a discount off an excursion, discounts off the full price of hairdressing and spa treatments, and also off portrait and standard size photographs, it's certainly worth joining.

(Since writing the above, P&O announced the launch of The Portunus Club which replaces the POSH Club, but I've left the paragraph in so you'll understand what seasoned cruisers are talking about when they mention the POSH Club – we do rather get set in our ways, and many of us still refer to it by its old name! Membership is automatic following your first cruise with P&O and points are awarded for each night spent on board qualifying you for different levels of discounts on board according to whether you are a Ruby, Sapphire or

Gold Member. All far too confusing for a brain still trying to organise itself following our last cruise in time for the next one, but Himself says it is a much simpler system, and doesn't require an annual membership fee.)

Which reminds me... have you seen your photographs yet? Can you see the difference between the one taken as you boarded in Southampton, all harassed and stressed, and the one at the Captain's Welcome Aboard party? Tonight, those of us with invitations to the drinks, will be asked to smile for another one as we stand at the entrance between Captain Walters and Staff Captain David Box.

So many handsome men in dinner jackets or tuxedos, along with the occasional dark suit, but it's the ladies who shine tonight. Those ladies who like sunbathing are positively glowing, and many figure hugging dresses are in evidence. Formal nights, like this evening, are as easy or as difficult as you wish to make them. There are many of the long black skirt and fancy top brigade, several evening trouser suits right up to the elegant 'My Fair Lady' outfit, complete with elbow length gloves. Although I have to confess, I only saw one pair of those tonight. They are not exactly high fashion with lady POSH Club members.

"He's there again!" I nudge Himself, and quickly look the other way.

"Where?" he hisses.

"Over there," I say, as I do my best inconspicuously to point out the subject of the conversation.

"I knew it was him the first time I saw him. Fancy after all these years. I honestly thought he'd have passed on to that great cruise club in the sky. He was certainly old enough when we met him."

Himself gives me one of his looks. He's a little touchy

about age since he was given a free television licence some years ago.

"He's coming our way," I tug at Himself's elbow.

Saved by the announcement! "…and do have an *hilarious* evening on board *Aurora*."

"We will, we will," I mutter, grabbing Himself's hand and making a hasty exit to the dining room.

"I don't feel strong enough to do battle with Harold tonight."

5

CASTAWAYS AND CASUALTIES

Little wonder Satya looks surprised to find us dressed when he arrives with our breakfast – we have already developed a reputation for moving slowly in the mornings – 'slithering like slugs' describes our top speed. Today is a sea day, a wonderful, peaceful, lazy day with no port to worry about, and no deadlines to meet. Today it is just the two of us, able to do as we please.

Except! At 11.00 a large percentage of the passengers will make their way to the Curzon Theatre where one of the celebrities on board, Richard Baker OBE, will interview the Captain, and we don't want to miss that, or be knocked over in the stampede to get a seat.

The stage is set and we take our seats. Under a beach umbrella, two reclining chairs have been placed one either side of a small wooden table on which sit two cocktails of the day – today it's a Chocolate Banana containing Kahlua Liqueur, fresh banana and cream – on second thoughts, those on the stage look more like glasses of orange juice. A ship's wheel with two parrots attached, two palm trees their bases covered with sand-coloured towels, a sun bleached skull, a skull and cross-bones hat, and a barrel of rum. Three plastic seagulls are suspended overhead, one sways madly in the non-existent breeze making the audience laugh, the raucous sound of seagulls fills the theatre. It's easy to believe that we are indeed on a desert island and ready for *Aurora's* version of Desert Island Discs.

The castaways appear to applause from the audience.

"Would you like being on a desert island?" Richard Baker asks the Captain when they've made themselves comfortable and taken a sip from their drinks.

"Probably not as I like people, so I'd prefer not to be marooned, but at least on this desert island you can find a sun-bed!" he replies causing much laughter from the audience.

Every cruise I have been on, passengers are asked not to reserve sun-beds, and are told: "If a sun-bed is left for more than 30 minutes it is considered available for use by others". Of course passengers still do it, sometimes reserving one on the sunny side of the ship and one in the shade, and regrettably no action seems to be taken against them by the crew.

The Captain's choice of music is not quite to Richard Baker's classical taste! He has chosen music he really likes, that reminds him of people and places, and he doesn't pretend to be a classical music buff. *Jesus Christ Super Star, Bohemian Rhapsody,* and *Pin Ball Wizard! – I believe in Father Christmas,* and *Love Changes Everything.* He gains a lot of respect from the passengers, although personally I do query his choice of the *Titanic* Theme – as I've said before, some passengers are a bit touchy about the 'T' word.

We learn that his wife is on board with him for about half the cruises he does, and that he's a motor racing fanatic and wants to move to a house with a bigger garage. I wonder why? And when asked what he would take with him to the desert island, immediately replies, "My cabin steward!" Wouldn't we all?

I leave the Curzon Theatre quickly, the applause still ringing in my ears. I am due elsewhere.

* * * * *

Cruise ships are divided into different sections – where passengers may go, and where they may not. We are all on holiday. We are here to relax and enjoy ourselves, and few if any of the passengers will give much thought to where anything they use, eat or drink comes from or goes to, and certainly don't care about the logistics of getting that item into a situation where they may use it, eat it, or drink it.

Occasionally you see a member of the crew disappearing through a door marked "Crew Only". In the Captain's safety announcement after embarkation, we were told not to enter these areas, even if invited to do so. Beyond these doors are found the working parts of the ship – the below stairs of a land based hotel. Beyond these doors is where the crew members work, relax, eat and sleep, where the food is prepared, where the huge piles of laundry are dealt with, the engine room, garbage areas and stores. *Aurora* does not resemble an iceberg, but there is a tremendous amount out of sight beyond the passenger areas.

Escorted by Geoff Stephenson, Hotel Services Stores Manager, half an hour 'below stairs' left me utterly amazed. Obviously the storage space was always going to be large – you only have to see the quantities of food we consume – but just how large I could never have imagined. I have since bought a video of 'below stairs' which any passenger can buy, but even that doesn't show the true size of the storage areas that extend to two decks of the ship.

When the ship docks in Southampton at the end of a cruise, the stores for the next cruise immediately start to come aboard through a huge opening in the side of the ship from where an adjustable platform extends – this provisioning will carry on all day. Stores come onto the ship in pallets and are moved around on one of the small fleet of miniature fork lift trucks – for our trip approximately 15 tons of meat, 4 tons of fish, 7 tons of poultry and game, 3.5 tons of bacon, ham and gammon, and 28 tons of fresh fruit and vegetables will be needed. 51,000 eggs, 10,500 litres of milk, 4,000 litres of ice cream, a bottle or two of alcohol and several four packs of beer, plus about seven pallets of toilet rolls, napkins, tissues etc. Most of P&O's cruises will be provisioned in the same way, with only small items bought abroad. On a world cruise containers of dried foods are shipped out to San Francisco, Australia and New Zealand, Singapore and Hong Kong to replenish the ship as she progresses around the world.

Although Geoff told me the storage rooms, all labelled with their contents, would be absolutely full at the commencement of a world cruise, the amount contained within them for this trip was massively impressive. The freezer rooms and chiller rooms are vast, and the dry stores space immense. The equivalent of a small dining room full to the ceiling of loo rolls! There's a separate freezer room for poultry, one for beef and lamb, another for pork and game.

The label on the door says ' Ice Blocks'.

"Don't you make them on board?" I ask naively.

"That's ice blocks for the ice carvings." Geoff replies as he opens the lock on the door. Alongside several large oblong blocks of ice, already stand a flower basket, a swan and an eagle, all hand carved by a Philippino from the galley who is employed for his ice carving abilities. Somehow the words 'ice' and 'Philippines' don't sit comfortably together. Did he originally practise on palm tree wood, I wonder?

Ordering all these stores is done well in advance of course – it's no good ringing Tesco's or Sainsbury's the morning you arrive in port. At least 14 days' notice is given for most stores, and the ship will carry three weeks' supply of stores for a two week cruise. Cornflour, horseradish, powdered milk, food colours and flavours, you name it, they've got it – in quantity.

There's a Herb Room where the smell of basil, thyme, and rosemary is overpowering – but I'm told that very strong flavours are kept separately!

The Dairy Room for the eggs and yoghurts, powdered egg yolks for scrambled eggs, Long Life milk and cream, and seven days' supply of fresh milk. No fresh milk is picked up elsewhere on our cruise because of quality control.

Thirty different cheeses are kept on board, some just for cooking.

Dry stores for the rice and flour – 8.9 tons of flour for this cruise. The bakers on board *Aurora* make bread for the whole ship, crew and passengers, every day – on this cruise 3,600 loaves of bread, 70,000 bread rolls and 42,000 afternoon cakes and pastries.

Bananas separated into first, second and third use, in varying stages of ripeness, are apparently the most difficult food item to store.

The salad stores where lettuces, tomatoes and cucumbers are kept at a normal fridge temperature of four degrees Celsius. Although they do use some frozen vegetables, there are plenty of fresh vegetables in evidence.

Boxes of avocado pears left out to ripen.

"Put a kiwi fruit with them to hasten ripening," said Geoff.

And on past the Butter and Oil room.

A room for Disposables, loo rolls in packs of 36 – always white – paper hand towels for the cloakrooms, face tissues, disposable gloves for the chefs, napkins, and even cake boards for the large cakes, never slimming, that emerge from the galley.

We're getting on to the interesting things… a room containing wine, bottled water and Champagne and another for the keg beer storage, soft drinks and cans of beer. Another for spirits and liqueurs!

"You use a lot of that?" I ask, pointing to several unopened cases of apricot brandy.

"A legacy left by the previous Stores Manager," Geoff answered my question.

Do you remember the Sea Breeze Cooler I drank on Monday, the alcoholic Drink of the Day? That contained apricot brandy! To shift the number of cases of it I saw, they'll have to find some other way of enticing passengers to drink it. It's not a popular after dinner drink… but I wonder what it would be like on ice cream?

What's this? A vast microwave, large enough to put you in and possibly me too at the same time! It sits in a room, all by itself.

"I normally only use it to take the frost off the meat or poultry," the guy who operates this monster of microwaves tells me.

"It speeds up the actual defrosting," he continues, "although in an emergency I can, of course, totally defrost anything in this microwave."

I leave the room thinking 'megawave' rather than microwave.

After the frost has been removed, the food is taken across the passageway to the defrosting room, where it sits in specially designed stainless steel trays until it is fully thawed.

There is a tremendous amount of stainless steel on this ship.

And on to the food preparation areas, which is all done well away from the galleys, where veal escalopes for this evening's dinner are being prepared by three men as we walk past.

There's a vegetable preparation area with a humongous potato-peeling machine – and one guy stands all day, every day for nine months, just taking the eyes out of the potatoes after they've been peeled in this machine. Hard to see which way his career will go. Potatoes are divided into new, regular and baking – the chips are already chipped before they're brought on board – what a pity that, I think. Wouldn't the 'de-eyeing guy' like a change of scenery and spend some time cutting spuds into chips?

And so, we have all this food being consumed, and to follow the process logically, obviously there must be waste. So what happens to that?

Waste food is ground down – except for fats as they would float – and put overboard outside coastal waters – that means 12 miles off shore in the Mediterranean. Broken china and glass is pulverised – a wonderful word that perfectly describes the reduction of all the items to fine gravel which is then discharged, returning to the sea bed to form sand… and what is a major constituent of glass? Sand! It's good to know that recycling is taking place whilst we are relaxing. Paper and plastics are sorted and burned. Garbage on a ship is a big operation and a 24-hour job. Three men are employed to do nothing but sort all the garbage on this ship. I honestly think, even wearing strong rubber gloves, that I'd rather de-eye the potatoes.

And finally, in our tour below stairs, we walk past the Engine Control Room, where someone is on watch all the time.

"What, no large wooden wheel?" I comment.

"No! It's all done with the touch of a mouse these days!"

So, before we climb back to the passenger accommodation areas, and in case anyone out there wants a job like his, I asked Geoff how he reached this position where he has an Assistant Manager and eight staff.

"Thirty-three years in the Royal Navy before I retired and joined P&O," was the answer.

For anyone who doesn't feel the urge to have a career in Her Majesty's Forces before joining P&O, get yourself a degree in Hotel Management, or a Catering degree or even experience in catering on shore. Around 120 chefs work in the galleys – but we'll come to that in a later chapter. For now it's amazing how hunger catches up with me! I have a date with Himself in a restaurant.

* * * * *

"Ladies and Gentlemen," the Captain's voice interrupts our lunch. "One of your fellow passengers has been taken ill and is in need of urgent medical treatment ashore. We have therefore arranged to rendezvous with the Majorcan Rescue Craft, which is exercising to the south of the island. I will keep you informed of developments."

Life afloat is like this, and occasionally itineraries are changed slightly to meet any unforeseen emergency. On board there are wonderful medical facilities and the doctors and nurses will happily deal with virtually anything the passengers can offer them. However, on occasions, and today is an example of this, the Senior Doctor feels that it is in the patient's interest to get him or her to a hospital on shore as quickly as possible.

Looking at the age of some of the passengers, it is really surprising that more of these sudden diversions don't occur. Today is a sea day, and all this really means to us is a trip towards the harbour at Palma, as the Majorcan Rescue Craft has been unable to transfer the patient on his stretcher in complete safety. It has therefore been decided to make a further detour and wait outside the entrance to the harbour, when one of our lifeboats will be used to take the patient to the jetty.

And before you imagine the patient strapped to a stretcher, lowered down a rope ladder, nothing could be further from what actually happens. On his stretcher he is very carefully placed into one of our lifeboats, which is then gently lowered to water level. It departs and is quickly on its way to the harbour side, where the patient is transferred smoothly into the waiting ambulance. I know it is a gentleman, not only because word gets around on a ship, but also because as Himself and I are leaving Café Bordeaux, the 24-hour Bistro where we have just enjoyed a quiet lunch, we are able to see him being put into the lifeboat. He looks remarkably cheerful considering he has had a major heart attack and is smiling at the crew around him… and he departs with the good wishes of every passenger watching the procedure from the Promenade Deck.

"Ladies and Gentlemen," the Captain's voice breaks into my thoughts. "I am sure you'll all be pleased to know that the patient is already in hospital in Palma and I'll keep you in touch with his progress. Our lifeboat is safely stowed back on board and we are now resuming our cruise around the north side of Majorca. Enjoy your afternoon on board."

Already, the impressive view of Palma's Gothic cathedral is fading into the distance as the Captain puts his foot down and we pick up speed. Many of the passengers are enjoying a BarBQ lunch on the aft deck of the Orangery, where the Pennant Bar waiters are serving jugs of Sangria – after all, we are in Spanish coastal waters.

Now I don't want you to think that all passengers are ghoulish and stand and stare at another's misfortune, like motorway drivers who slow down to gaze at an accident on the opposite carriageway. There is a special camaraderie that builds up very quickly on a cruise between everyone on board, passengers and crew, and there will be many on board who either know the patient or his wife, or know someone who knows someone who knows him! We are all concerned for him and his speedy recovery. Add to this the fact that virtually everyone who cruises loves the sea and everything to do with it, so being able to watch an unscheduled lifeboat launch gives added interest to the day.

So yes, some may think it ghoulish, but to us happy cruisers, we're just being ourselves, showing a healthy interest in all that goes on in our floating hotel, and as we're mostly very experienced sailors by now and know *everything* about cruise ships, we're also keeping an eye on the Captain and crew too, in case they should need our help! It's not just the weather we're good at looking after!

Not all emergencies are as easy to cope with as this afternoon's, and not all patients are able to smile. I can remember two occasions when seriously ill passengers had to be air lifted from the ship by helicopter in an effort to get them to land based hospitals even more quickly. In these cases, passengers were not allowed onto the open decks, and even balcony cabin occupants were evacuated. On one occasion, the dining room was also emptied until the helicopter had left the area of the ship. It's a delicate operation winching a passenger in a stretcher off an open deck, and you can imagine what havoc could be caused to other passengers and the ship, should there be an accident with the helicopter. A helicopter pilot needs all his concentration and distractions caused by camera flashes from passengers determined to record every moment of the transfer, could have fatal consequences.

So now, the excitement is over. Let's settle back and enjoy the next few hours as we follow the coastline of Majorca. Luckily for us, we are going clockwise around the island, which means those of us who have starboard side balconies need do nothing more than literally watch the world go by.

Majorca is so much more than just the crowded resorts in the south near to Palma and the bikini clad resorts on the east coast. The west coast from Isla Dragonera up to Cabo Formentor is magnificent with high cliffs plunging into the sea, and there is no better way to appreciate them than lounging on a balcony with a drink in hand, binoculars at the ready.

We're sailing past Banyalbufar, where over the years the villagers have terraced the hillside. Look at the small beach below. Close your eyes – can't you just imagine the smugglers landing there, many years ago?

Puerto Soller, where the town is built around the circular bay, now gaining popularity and not as quiet as when we first visited almost 20 years ago.

On past Sa Calobra, a tiny seaside settlement, where man-made tunnels through the solid rock lead to the mouth of the Twin Torrents – a massive ravine, whose mouth is visible to us from the sea, and which has been carved into the land by the endless passage of winter torrents. It's a two and a half mile long prehistoric gorge that can only be walked through in the summer months, and only then if the torrent is completely dry. It takes between four and five hours to pass through the ravine one way so don't forget you have to thumb a lift back to collect your transport!

"Ah. Formentor," Himself stirs.

"Ah yes, I remember it well," I break into song. We spent ten glorious days in the isolated hotel favoured by the rich and famous, including Winston Churchill – and the not so rich like us – reached by a narrow road that descends steeply around endless hairpin bends.

"Shall we go back?" I ask.

"You can't have your cruises and Formentor," Himself, ever practical, replies.

"No contest!" I answer.

"Look at the dolphins," Himself cries.

"They're playing!"

I lower the binoculars from scanning the steep cliffs and watch as a school of dolphins plays in the calm waters. Do dolphins play? Well they certainly appear to at times, and I'd rather not think about them shopping for supper on a superbly soporific afternoon like this.

Bing Bong! "Good evening Ladies and Gentlemen. Dinner is now being served in the Alexandria and Medina Restaurants. Do have an *idyllic* evening on board *Aurora*."

But we have two more hours before dinner, when we'll have a *joyous* evening on board *Aurora*. The joys of second sitting!

A ring at the door and I answer it – yes, along with the use of binoculars for the duration of your stay on board, you do get a doorbell in a suite! Well, you'd hardly expect our visitors to have to hammer on the door, would you?

A tall, handsome, ginger-haired man wearing shorts, and with athletic looking hairy legs stands there with a bottle of champagne and two glasses in his hands.

For a moment I think I've died and gone to Heaven!

He asks for me by name, and when I've said "yes", with a smile introduces himself.

"I'm Andrew Laycock, MD of Cruise Options." This is the specialist Travel Agent through whom we booked the cruise, and Andrew is on board with his wife, Sarah, and their young son Lewis.

"Hope you're enjoying the cruise, and that this will help you," he says, handing me the bottle and glasses.

"What a wonderful surprise!" I say when I've got my breath back. "Thank you very much indeed," and, calling Himself, ask Andrew to bring his wife to our suite so that we can all enjoy his generous gift.

* * * * *

For the first evening on the cruise, we are not the last table to leave the dining room, as we want to make sure of getting seats in the theatre.

"What a perfect day," Mr F.T.C. is obviously happy.

"Heaven knows why it's taken us so long to do this," Mrs F.T.C. is happy too.

"This just gets better and better," she carries on. "Wonderful weather, wonderful scenery, delicious dinner, amusing company, and now this excellent concert. What could be more perfect?"

I will add that as we passed Carmen's the Pop Explosion was in full swing – noisily of course, and people were standing knee deep in Champions Bar. The Syndicate Quiz was just starting in Vanderbilts, and there was a long queue of people going into the Cinema to see *The Hours*. So not everyone on board was enjoying the Opera Evening, although the Theatre was almost full.

Can today get any better? Possibly not, but there's always tomorrow to try!

6

AJACCIO – MAQUIS & MOUNTAINS

I hope you had a good night's sleep last night! I meant to warn you – today is the first of five consecutive days of port visits, and as such they'll be tiring. No doubt by the last one, you'll see why a lot of passengers, me included, prefer the days when *Aurora* is at sea.

Here in Ajaccio – pronounced Ajaxio – on the island of Corsica, it is somewhere Himself and I have not visited before, so we have booked a trip, or excursion.

P&O, along with most cruise lines, offers a bewildering array of shore excursions – bewildering mainly to the first time cruisers – and Mr and Mrs F.T.C. are indeed spoilt for choice and undecided which trip to choose.

"But you've been there before," a friend said to me when I told her we were going to Barcelona on this cruise. What she doesn't appreciate is that after a few cruises, the ports often become almost incidental. Enjoyment of the ship and life afloat is the real holiday and sometimes, in fact, the interruption and requirement to get off and do something becomes an irritant.

I've lost count of the number of times I've been to Barcelona, but it's a huge place and no matter how often we visit, there is always something to interest us. A tour of the city including the Church of La Sagrada Familia, a trip to Park Güell, the Spanish Village, Olympic Stadium, the Cactus Gardens, Botanical Gardens, the list is almost endless. Once we even enjoyed a visit to see the Black Madonna of Montserrat, the Benedictine monastery in the jagged mountains a couple of hours inland from Barcelona. On this cruise there are 13 different excursions to tempt passengers, including Golf, Fantasy Island Waterpark, FC Barcelona for budding David Beckhams and a tour of Barcelona on bicycle. There must be something there to interest most people.

Imagine visiting London for a day and then returning some months later for another day. Cruising is like this, and when you feel you've had your fill of scenery, culture and the surrounding area, you can always resort to shopping, an art form in itself, or even just enjoy a romantic lunch in some pavement café, jug of Sangria on the table, eye on your watch, of course, to ensure you catch the last shuttle bus back to the ship.

I digress, as you've probably realised by now I am prone to do. Shuttle bus! These are organised by the Shore Excursion Office from where tickets can be purchased. These shuttle buses ferry passengers from the quayside to a central point in the town or city being visited and will collect from the same spot to return passengers to the ship.

A list of all excursions is sent to your home address about six weeks before sailing date. You then have a choice. You can book by phone or by filling in the accompanying form. All excursion costs are added to your on board account in the case of P&O.

However, if you don't want to commit yourself to an excursion so far in advance, you can of course book on board at the Excursion Office, but do be warned that some trips are very popular and sell out quickly, and there are occasions when disappointment may follow if you try to book too late. For instance, the last bookings for tomorrow's trips to Livorno, Florence and Pisa had to be made by 18.00 yesterday afternoon. All deadline details can be found in *Aurora Today*.

You can, of course, get off the ship and 'do your own thing'. I know several people who hate to be organised and either potter by themselves or hire a taxi and visit somewhere possibly not offered by the Excursion Office. We have done all combinations of the above. You can even stay just where you are and enjoy an almost empty cruise ship.

However, today we're visiting somewhere new to us and so I've booked us all on Tour B, entitled Mountains and Maquis which will take us deep into the Corsican countryside. So why not come along and enjoy the scenery?

Ajaccio is a tender port and in *Aurora Today* we have been told to go to the Curzon Theatre by 09.15 at the latest. Three tours leave at 09.15, one at 09.30 and one at 09.40. As you can imagine, the Theatre is heaving – there could be in excess of seven or eight hundred people to process quickly.

On entering the Theatre we show our tickets – you did remember to bring them – and are each given a round sticker with our Tour and Coach number – B2. It is important not to lose these stickers and to wear them somewhere visible. If you get lost on a tour, and it has been known, it makes it easier for the guide to find you. Also you should take a note of the telephone number of the Ship's Agent in Ajaccio. This is especially important if you've decided to do your own exploring and find you need help because of any problem, accident, or even an over zealous pickpocket! And do make sure you are back on board at least half an hour before sailing.

Cruise lines run to scheduled times, and 1,868 passengers will not be delayed because one couple has decided to venture a little too far in a taxi that has run out of petrol! If you have a problem, get in touch with the Agent who will tell the ship. You can always fly on to the next port and catch us up there. Don't laugh! It has happened!

"B2 please follow Karen who will take you to the tender," the young officer announces.

Our group has been called and it's a brisk walk down to where we get on the tender, pausing only to say a quick "Good Morning" to Neil, the Senior First Officer, who is looking very official today as he oversees the tender operation. We'll have to tell him tonight at dinner just how organised and smoothly run the whole operation was.

Here follows a short but bouncy boat ride and then we're on the quayside in Ajaccio and climbing onto our air-conditioned coach. So settle back and enjoy the commentary.

When asked the distance between two points on Corsica, the answer will be given in time, not kilometres, because of the terrain. The answer in kilometres may be quite short, but the time taken to cover those kilometres may not be.

Our coach is already winding its way along a steep sided valley and our guide, an English lady who, years ago, with her husband and then young family, sold up their home and bought a catamaran intending to spend a year afloat. They fell in love with Corsica and never left, but their children have long since flown the nest. Even following her husband's death a few years ago, she stayed, accompanying tours and writing books in her spare time, including one on the flowers of Corsica which are profuse. So naturally her English is excellent, which is good for us. Sometimes the guide is pretty fluent in English, but with such a heavy local accent that I spend most of my time trying to decipher what has been said, and almost missing whatever it is that it has been said about!

We are heading for the mountains, but already the maquis is all around us. This is the name given to the verdant natural vegetation that covers Corsica – made up of arbutus, myrtle, honeysuckle, cistus, fennel, thorn, laurel, brook, thyme, rosemary and lavender. It is also the name given to the French resistance movement that fought against the Germans in World War II, from the idea of the thick vegetation providing cover for resistance members hiding in the hills.

Napoleon, who was born in Corsica, was supposed to have said he could smell the island before he saw it as he returned from a journey abroad. Can you smell the perfume? Sometimes it is quite heady as it wafts across the vegetation in the morning sun.

In the woodland all around are wild boar weighing up to 100 kilos (Himself tells me that's 225lbs or approximately 16 stone) – they know they're safe at the moment because the hunting season is August to early February. Every village has a boar hunt each year and a total of 15,000 are killed – or culled – throughout the island. It's enough to put you off gammon for life.

Sometimes the wild boar mate with domestic pigs and the resultant piglets are eventually released into the wild. In the woods there are also wild mushrooms, so anyone who decides to go mushrooming between August and early February, should wear bright colours and make a lot of noise – wild boar hunters have often killed mushroom pickers by accident.

Until the Second World War, most Corsicans lived in the mountain villages where they were safer from invasion by sea and also away from the mosquitoes which carried a fatal form of malaria. Along came the Americans who wanted to build a runway, sprayed the whole area with D.D.T., and killed off the mosquitoes and all other insects too. Malaria disappeared, as did the birds, now having no food. Nowadays the majority of Corsicans live near to the coast – and the birds have returned too.

The government is offering financial help to the young people to encourage them to repopulate the interior as mountain guides, shepherds, foresters and to open small hotels. Tourism is very important and hotels are invariably fully booked for the summer by early spring.

Can you smell the pine trees? These Corsican Pines, 40 metres high and with trunks two metres in diameter, used to be sold for sailing ship masts, but the wood is now exported to make furniture. I forgot to mention, *Aurora* doesn't have a mast – she has a massive funnel painted egg yolk yellow!

Apparently Corsica abounds with wildlife – we look this way and that on the coach in an effort to spot this wildlife – apart from the wild boars, there are wild sheep too, red deer, eagles, osprey and bearded vultures, although with the thick pine forests and all encompassing maquis, we'll have to take our guide's word for their presence.

We've arrived at the top of the Prunelli Gorge – it's a very, very narrow road that unbelievably was widened only last year! Although supposedly two-way, it's barely wide enough for the coach in places. I don't want to think about what will happen if we meet another vehicle, the sharp edges of the cutaway rock walls are but a few inches from the window and my head.

"You can have the window seat after our coffee break," I cheerfully inform Himself!

The sun is blazing down as we stop for refreshments near the lake of Tolla, a reservoir that was man-made in 1956 and provides water and hydroelectric power for Ajaccio and all the villages in between.

OK, so you can do most of these trips by yourself in a taxi, but would you learn so much about the country you are visiting and would you be able to see as much from lower down in your car or taxi? Would you be told that until recently you could build a family tomb on your own land – the tombs here in Corsica look like small houses with Cypress trees towering above them.

Sweet chestnuts, called the Tree of Life or Bread Tree by the Corsicans as they provide sustenance from the cradle to the grave, used to be the staple diet of the Corsicans, but are now eaten by pigs in winter. However, there are approximately 35,000 hectares of chestnut forest and the locals have now started milling chestnut flour and making cakes and biscuits from it.

Corsican honey is exceptional and we are told it is the only honey in the world to be given the Appellation Contrôlée label – hardly surprising when I think of all the blooms we have seen today. I knew the French awarded the Appellation Contrôlée to some wines, but didn't realise that some foods were also given it. Now would you have learned that information by yourselves?

And finally, Estée Lauder has a distillery on Corsica to produce essential oils because the plants are pure and there is no pollution – except for our coach fumes of course!

As we drive back to Ajaccio through a valley full of market gardens, past figs and olives, citrus, kumquat, clementines, greengages and plums, it is easy to see why our guide and her late husband fell in love with the island.

As usual, we have only scratched the surface, but who knows, a cruise next year may bring us back to this beautiful island, when we'll be able to explore a little more.

Do you feel it yet? That unmistakeable feeling of relief! That feeling of coming home! We've enjoyed our excursion, but the comfort and cool of *Aurora* beckons.

The afternoon evaporates as afternoons on board tend to do. By the time we've enjoyed another leisurely lunch in Café Bordeaux, Himself is ready to produce some *stentorian* snores of Olympic medal winning proportions. We were, after all, up early this morning, much to Satya's surprise.

Himself doesn't hear the canapés arrive – deep fried courgettes and cream cheese in breadcrumbs today – or even when I pour a gin and tonic and return to the cool of the balcony now in the shade, but only arouses when the faithful are called for early dinner and told to have a *knowledgeable* evening on board! I wonder if the Restaurant Manager is referring to the Syndicate Quiz?

The sun is setting as we sail away from Corsica having safely gathered all our ducklings back on board for the night.

* * * * *

Tonight at dinner we learn some sad news.

"It's not been a good day," says Neil, when he joins us for dinner. "We've lost a passenger!"

No, before you ask, we didn't leave him behind on Corsica – sadly he died during the night. This is, after all, a story about cruising, and contains information on a myriad of subjects. Regrettably, death is just one of them and something we all have to face, eventually. I should be grateful to the unknown passenger, a gentleman travelling alone, as his demise has introduced another subject to be expanded upon.

"I'm sure he didn't do it on purpose," I say with a straight face. "And I can't think of a better place to be when it happens to me," I add.

So, what do we do? Parcel him up into a bin bag and dispose of him at sea? In the old, old days, probably yes, but not today with modern feelings about conservation and pollution. To be quite blunt about it, the mortuary on board can cater for five people, and on a two week cruise, as on this occasion, the deceased will often be carried all the way round and taken off the ship in Southampton. The paperwork is immense. I sometimes wonder why paperwork for anything in this modern world has to be so onerous. Surely with progress and computerisation, paperwork should be reduced. It would appear not to be so.

So, two people on board have my sympathy, the steward who unfortunately couldn't wake his passenger when he took in his early morning tea, and Neil who has spent the greater part of today escaping from endless forms.

I don't sound sad? Possibly because I've heard it all

before but more likely because I know that a man who doesn't really enjoy cruising would never come on a cruise by himself. I have no knowledge of his home circumstances, but I wouldn't mind betting that he's now reunited with a late adored wife who probably also had webbed feet.

By virtue of the age and medical condition of some of the passengers, a death on board is not an unheard of occurrence. It's just that passengers don't often get to hear the details, although, as I've already said, word travels fast on the ship's telegraph!

On a world cruise, repatriation would take place sooner – it would be unreasonable to expect P&O to carry its departed passenger round through the Panama, Pacific, around New Zealand and Australia, the Far East and the Suez Canal. I'm just sad that he died last night, and not on the last day of the cruise by which time he would have enjoyed some magnificent scenery and warm sunshine.

Cruising is a wonderful way for single people to enjoy safe holidays where they need never be alone unless they want to be so. It would be almost impossible for even the shyest person not to make friends on a cruise. In the dining room, theatre, on excursions, walking around the deck, the occasions and opportunities to meet people are frequent.

By virtue of the age difference between us, and all things being equal, Himself and I both know that I will probably end my days cruising around the world in ever decreasing circles. No housework, no cooking, no need to be lonely, excellent medical care on board, and plenty of first class entertainment! What more could a young at heart OAP want? After all, I have a good example to follow.

We met dear Kay on the last trip of the *Canberra* and have maintained contact ever since. Not a youngster in 1997, she celebrated her 90th birthday in Cape Town on *Oriana's* 2003 World Cruise. She told me that during the day she'd been taken up Table Mountain by some of the crew and her friends, where they'd all had a meal. Having had a wonderful party on board, at nearly midnight she and several friends then went ashore again to visit the night clubs and didn't get back until 05.00. She only arrived back in England in the April, but immediately booked a cruise to Norway in June, hoped to do the New England USA cruise at the end of August, and had a cabin booked for the Christmas and New Year cruise on *Aurora*. It is a case of *use it or lose it* and Kay obviously has no intention of losing it yet a while!

Life on board ship is not as expensive as one would think, and taking a cabin lower down the ship suits Kay very well – it's obviously slightly cheaper, but also more stable in 'lumpy' seas. She uses her cabin for sleeping and little else, and the rest of the time she's happily occupied on the ship.

So – how shall be spend our *laudable* evening on board *Aurora* tonight? There is a Great British Pub Night in Champions' Bar, The Aurora Theatre Company proudly present their Movie World Show, shall we watch a Hugh Grant film in the Playhouse, or listen to a Violin and Piano Recital? We could go dancing in Carmens, be intelligent in Vanderbilts and join a table for the Syndicate Quiz, or maybe go for a quiet drink and chat in the Crow's Nest?

Or maybe, just maybe, we should have an early night, just the two of us!

7

A.B.C. & A.B.T.
Part One

"Come on – do hurry up, or you'll miss it!"

Yes, indeed, we're off again, and you'll now begin to understand why cruising can be hard work. During the night whilst we slept – eventually – the crew very kindly moved the ship from Corsica to Livorno. This is one of the real joys of cruising, being able to visit so many different places, but only packing your suitcases once, invariably with great regret, at the end of the cruise.

Livorno. Haven't you heard of it? Well it's towards the top of the western coast of Italy, not a seaside resort, but a major naval base and, more importantly for Himself and me, it's the port you use if you want to visit Pisa and Florence by sea.

Where shall we go? Well in the past we've visited both Pisa and Florence several times, but having spent a couple of weekends in Florence at the beginning of our marriage, it holds a very special place in our hearts. As it's a place a great many of you will no doubt have visited before, I thought I'd give you a treat and send you all on a quick trip which Himself and I did in 1991, just after the first Gulf War. And just to make sure you know what you're looking at, I've prepared this commentary to accompany your virtual reality tour. So here you go, on a Trip to the Nile.

This may well be exceptional use of poetic licence, but if you jump onto my magic carpet and close your eyes, I'll wave a magician's wand and transport you there. Have a nice day and see you back here on *Aurora* in time to change for dinner – and don't be late!

* * * * *

It was the 16th December – 06.00. David, my sister's *little* boy (6'2" and nearly 17) was revelling in an extra week off school and our son John, newly home from boarding school was re-checking his rucksack for all the essentials a ten year old seemed to need to take to Egypt! Himself and I sat quietly in the car – we were too old even then for early mornings!

Our flight to Luxor went smoothly – in fact better than normal as David had taken on the job of nanny and was trying to persuade John that the in-flight meal really was edible, despite the fact there was a lack of fish fingers, baked beans and toasted cheese. A video and endless pop music kept them both quiet and for once Himself and I could doze and imagine what miles of sand would really look like, the effects of the in-flight liquid refreshment having gently dulled the sound of the aircraft noise.

Regrettably, by the time we arrived at Luxor airport, it was almost dark as being so much nearer to the

Equator the nights start much earlier and much more suddenly too. Don't blink, or you'll miss the twilight we experience in the UK. Although the sunsets are wonderful, once the sun has gone, it's absolutely dark.

We were met by Tarek, our guide – mid-twenties, with a Lebanese mother and a Syrian father, who spoke virtually perfect English, German and French and, of course, Arabic too. He studied Ancient Egyptian History at university and was a very handsome young man, who would be with us for the whole week and would in that time fill us all with enthusiasm for temples and help us to understand some of the history of the people who lived in the narrow strip of fertile land on both sides of the life-giving River Nile.

A short drive through the outskirts of Luxor and we arrived at the *m.s. RA*, our Nile cruiser and home for the next seven days. Nowadays there are so many river cruisers taking holiday-makers up and down the Nile, that it is impossible for them all to moor next to the bank. To solve this problem they tie up alongside each other, sometimes four or five ships away from the bank and to reach the shore you just walk from your ship, through the next, and the next, and so on, until you reach the final gangplank. If one of the ships in between decides to leave, everyone else casts off, lets the ship out, and ties up again, one ship nearer to the shore! A sort of maritime shuffle.

We'd seen pictures of the *m.s. RA*, built only a couple of years earlier, but we weren't prepared for the inside. Reception was on the gangplank level (here we are talking a real gangplank, and nothing like the elaborate steps down which you left *Aurora* this morning) and the dining room was one floor down, which meant your feet were actually below the water level. At times during the cruise, the water would splash against the eye level windows as we were eating, giving a very strange sensation. It was a large dining room easily able to cater for the 120 passengers the ship can carry, with a few tables for four people, but mostly tables seating eight.

The floor above Reception is where all the cabins are to be found and the one above that holds the remaining cabins, the shop and bar-cum-lounge. Above everything is a large sun deck, partially covered to give shade, and including an icy cold swimming pool – or at least it was according to David and John – very few of us 'oldies' tried it out, prepared to accept their judgement! It's a very comfortable boat, well organised and very efficiently run. The rooms were always maintained beautifully, the laundry service was speedy and extremely good and cheap, and regrettably the food was delicious and far too fattening just before Christmas.

We met Tarek in the lounge for a welcome chat where he explained the itinerary you will be following. However, he did add one piece of important information, so please absorb the following.

"I know that rumours abound about dreadful diarrhoea, dysentery, and general stomach problems caused by eating the food on board," Tarek announced to the lounge full of long faces. "Worry not!" he added. "The only problems on this ship are caused by the passengers eating too much meat which lies and festers in their stomachs and causes major problems." And he put great emphasis on the word 'fester'.

"Eat sensibly the sort of amounts you'd eat at home, and there will not be a problem. The food, including the salads, is quite safe to eat."

I will say that despite predictions by John's Headmaster before we left the UK, none of us had a single problem, except one morning when David had indeed eaten vast quantities of meat the evening before, and he stayed on board and had to miss another temple. I certainly ate salad every day for lunch without any repercussions.

Having unpacked, eaten dinner, remembering Tarek's warning of course, and briefly explored the boat, we settled down for a good night's sleep, knowing that the ship would sail north during the night and that in the morning we would see our first temple.

We were told we'd have a wake-up call at 07.00, breakfast would be at 07.30 and we'd be on the coach at 08.00. For the only time, I felt as though I was back at school, being organised to the minute, and half wondered, as I drifted off to sleep, whether this would be a success or not.

"That's a xylophone," Himself said, as we both woke with a start. Each and every morning one of the crew walked up and down the accommodation corridors going 'plink, plonk, plink, brrrrrrrrr, plink, plonk, plink' on his xylophone. It was far more romantic than the old alarm clock, and quite insistent enough. There was movement in the next cabin, so even David and John were awake – I didn't think teenagers ever woke in the mornings. Quickly down to breakfast and then on to the coach, a routine that was repeated most mornings with an ease and cheerfulness which made you forget it was all organised.

DENDERA AND THE TEMPLE OF HATHOR. Some 48 kilometres north of Luxor lies Qena, capital of the province of the same name, and it is here you find the impressive Temple of Hathor, Goddess of love, joy and beauty, and the wife of the falcon God Horus, sometimes depicted as a woman with a cow's head. Dendera is a short coach-ride inland from the west bank of the Nile and seemed vast to our inexperienced eyes at this stage. Large parts are in ruins, but there is still so much to see and the couple of hours we had here were totally inadequate. Vast columns, endless hieroglyphics, a wall of mud bricks surrounding the whole temple area, a sacred lake and everywhere Hathor heads, a woman's head with cow's ears. It was here that we met God Bes, a dwarf God, who helped mothers in childbirth and was protector of new mothers and the newborn. He was also God of dance, music and pleasure – I couldn't quite see how he could combine the two jobs! We were to meet him several times over the next week.

By now you should be well on the way to the end of your first film! I certainly was as we returned to the coach and went back to the ship for lunch. Lunch on board was the best meal of the day consisting of a large buffet with European and Egyptian food, hot and cold, and a wonderful display of desserts, including fresh dates. We were encouraged to return for more, and more, and to try this and that, whilst, during lunch, the crew of the *m.s. RA* was smoothly transporting us to our next temple.

ABYDOS, AND THE TEMPLE OF SETI I. Abydos is the holiest place and goal of pilgrimages for untold centuries. It had the same significance for the ancient world as Mecca today. It is the place where Osiris is supposedly buried, and also the area that produced the kings of the first dynasties, leading to the unification of the upper and lower lands of Egypt.

It was the coach journey to Abydos that, for us tourists not as yet used to Egypt, was the interesting part, almost as much as the temple itself. The coach, air-conditioned of course, sped along modern roads, through sugar cane plantations, along the edge of channels fed by Nile water, past scenes straight from the Bible – and I mean the original, not the modern version. People carrying their loads on their heads, palm trees, flat topped mud huts, water buffalo, goats and sheep, men riding on donkeys, camels, ladies covered from head to toe in black, and men in their *galebeah* (long caftan-type garments) and everywhere the desert just in the background. Before this journey, I had no idea that the strip of inhabited and fertile land on both sides of the Nile is so narrow, less that half a mile in places, and the change from fertile, irrigated land to desert, so sudden and dramatic.

Tarek stopped the coach driver and bought some fresh sugar cane, which we all experienced as refreshment when we reached the temple.

I'm not a 'coach' person, but this journey was really well worth the time. The sights were so different to the normal European holiday and being high in the coach, we were able to appreciate the scenery in comfort – and be cool at the same time.

Abydos lies on the East Bank about 322 miles south of Cairo, and this was the furthest north we were to go on this trip. It is very confusing to start with as the River Nile rises in the south and ends up in the north at the Mediterranean. For some reason we all felt that going downstream we ought to be heading south, whereas in fact we were doing the opposite.

Osiris – God of Death and Resurrection – was murdered and dismembered. Poor chap! The myth goes on to say that various bits of his body were left in different locations and Abydos claimed to be the burial place of his head. A certain *member* was thrown into the Nile, which is the reason why, even today, many people on the banks of the river will not eat Nile fish! Funny lot, these Egyptians!

The temple was built by Seti I and finished off by his son, Ramesses II in approximately 1,300BC – obviously there wasn't a penalty clause in that building contract. It is said to be one of the most beautiful in Egypt, but is also of unusual design. It has seven sanctuaries, instead of the usual single one, and it is 'L' shaped. Most of the faces on the hieroglyphs in Dendera had been defaced by the Coptics (Christians), but many at Abydos had escaped the chisel.

Back to the coach – a sample of the fresh sugar cane which I didn't find refreshing, and the return journey to the *m.s. RA*. It had been a long first day, but it wasn't over yet. Following dinner, those with energy left played Bingo, whilst the rest of us sat quietly and relaxed as the boat began sailing through the night, upstream, towards Luxor.

THE VALLEY OF THE KINGS. Plink, plonk, plink, brrrrrrrr, plink, plonk, plink – that xylophone again.

"Not A.B.T.," came the scream from next door.

Breakfast: tied up at Luxor, and a ferry trip across the Nile to the West Bank, and onto the coach. The first stop of the morning was the Valley of the Kings. Now I don't know what I really expected, but it wasn't what I got! If you had been driving past by yourself, and had been able to remove the stall holders and people trying to sell you everything from a *galebeah* to a scarab beetle, a *genuine* hieroglyphic to a *genuine* replica of a *genuine* sacred black cat, I doubt you'd have realised anything was there. The story of Jesus throwing the moneychangers out of the temple came to mind!

The road to the Valley of the Kings runs northwards past Howard Carter's house – the man who discovered the Tomb of Tutankhamun in 1922 – the valley is secluded and contains some 62 excavated tombs (as in 1991), not all of these being of royal people, as privileged members of the nobility were also buried there. There are still believed to be many undiscovered tombs – a thought for anyone with a spare weekend or two. The entrances to the tombs are small and cut directly into the side of the cliffs.

The first tomb we went into was that of Ramesses XI which was long and narrow, and not only went into the mountain, but also went down quite steeply too. The walls and ceiling were decorated with wonderful hieroglyphics, all telling the story of Ramesses and the journey to 'the other side'. The burial chamber at the end of the vast corridor is dominated by the shattered remains of the massive granite sarcophagus which is said to have been broken into by thieves. This is one of the largest tombs in the valley.

Our second tomb was that of Ramesses III – there were a lot of these Ramesses – which had been begun for his father, Sethnakht, but abandoned because the corridor cut into the adjacent tomb of Amenmesses. Eventually a sharp right hand turn for twelve feet or so, allowed the corridor to be continued for Ramesses III – one might say it was a design fault, rather like coming across old sewers when digging foundations for new buildings today. These old Egyptians had a hard time of it – after all, we are talking of tunnelling through solid rock.

We were then offered a third tomb, for those who wanted to, but as young John said quietly to me: "Mum, if you *want* to go into another, I'll go with you, but honestly, when you've seen one tomb, you've seen 'em all."

Not quite true, but I did see his point, and the draw of the market stalls and bargains to be bartered for, had a strong pull, for him at least.

Regrettably, the tomb of Tutankhamun was closed at the time of our visit. Each tomb spends part of the year closed to allow it to dry out – the problem is caused by many hot bodies going through the tombs and creating moisture, which in turn causes mould and can ruin the hieroglyphics.

On now to the **VALLEY OF THE QUEENS** – a much smaller valley, but ringed by impressive cliffs and not only used for the royal ladies, but also for their sons too in some cases. Here we went into the tomb of Prince Khaemwaset, Ramesses III's eldest son. Quite different in design to previous tombs we had visited, it had six small rooms off the main corridor, three on either side.

"Come on! Hurry up! Back onto the coach! We still have lots to see today."

Another ride through the desert to the **TEMPLE OF QUEEN HATSHEPSUT.** Although magnificent to look at from a distance as it nestles into the cliff side, it is less spectacular on closer inspection. A lot of renovation work was being done and the upper level was closed. Queen Hatshepsut had the temple built opposite her burial chamber in the Valley of the Kings where she and her parents were to be worshipped. She also made it a 'Paradise for Amun', her favourite God, and to reinforce her throne on which she reigned for 33 years; a long time in those days.

Onwards now towards the **COLOSSI OF MEMNON** – two famous statues of King Amenhoep III, which once flanked the monumental entrance of the funerary temple of the Pharaoh. Each carved from a single block of very compact sandstone, both statues stand 51 feet high, on a base of 7.5 feet. They are *colossal* – sorry about that! Little remains of the temple and the statues now appear somewhat strange, as they stand on a vast, flat plain, in the middle of nowhere.

Except, that is, for the papyrus 'factory'. Across the road from the Colossi was a small building that turned out to be a papyrus *showroom*. In Biblical times, the papyrus was indeed made around here, but now it only grows in Northern Egypt, although they did have one rather sad looking papyrus plant growing outside, well watered, to show to the tourists. If it had been in your garden, you'd have been planning a trip to the garden centre in search of its replacement.

We were shown how the sacred plant is turned into papyrus paper. The outer skin is taken off and used for making baskets. The sliced papyrus is soaked in water for six days to remove the sugar and then it's rolled and woven and pressed for six more days. At the end of this a piece of papyrus paper is formed, very bendable and able to be written and painted on. We were then, of course, able to buy papyrus paintings of various shapes and designs – talk about captive tourists! We emerged with several, one of Tutankhamun, the Winged Scarab beetle, the Tree of Life, the Key of Life, and Nefertari – all of which are still awaiting frames, but they seemed like a good idea at the time.

We returned to the *m.s. RA* for another delicious lunch and a quiet afternoon before departing to the Temple of Karnak for a Sound and Light performance that evening. When the sun goes down and darkness appears the land of Egypt becomes quite different. For a start it's cooler, which is a blessing as, even in December in the heat of the day, it was very hot in the sun, but the magic of the desert by moonlight is shivery. As we strolled past the Ram Headed Sphinxes, through the Great Hypostyle Hall with the towering columns and on to the Sacred Lake of the Temple for the performance, I for one wouldn't have been surprised if we'd caught a fleeting glimpse of Amun-Ra – the God of the Sun. Was that a white-robed priest I saw in the moonlight?

Thursday morning, I'll spare you the xylophone but I'm sure you're awake, and echoes of

"Not A.B.C. and A.B.T." were heard from next door.

"A.B.C.?" I asked Himself.

He shrugged his shoulders and shook his head, a dangerous thing to do whilst shaving.

This morning, it's only a short coach trip to the **TEMPLE OF KARNAK,** which is on the outskirts of Luxor. This temple is vast and the largest we were to visit. It covers some 200 acres and consists of several temples and was built between 2,000BC and 51BC. In the daylight it lost a lot of the magical feeling of the night before.

But where do we start? Vast columns towering into the sky, a giant granite statue of Ramesses II, the Avenue of Ram Headed Sphinxes, the colossal Scarab, the Obelisk. There is too much to absorb, it's too vast to describe, and everywhere the feeling of following in the footsteps of the Pharaohs. Almost eerie! Legend has it that if you run around the Scarab beetle three times your fertility will be assured. The only member of our party to risk it was John, who at ten years old, felt safe!

It's no good. You'll never do it. We're only half way

through and there's still such a lot to see. I've organised the flights, and instead of returning to Pisa this evening to catch *Aurora*, you're going to stay with the Nile and fly back to Rome tomorrow evening.

Hope you're not too disappointed – you can always fly to Rome for a city break, but the Nile is magical, and it would be such a shame to miss A.B.T.

8

A.B.C. & A.B.T.
Part Two

We're off to do some shopping, the first of two shopping trips in Egypt.

Having left Karnak we were on our way to the temple at Luxor. Having been driven through the bustling city we were taken to a luxury hotel where we were able to use the spotless toilets – in Egypt, loos on the whole are not terribly, how can I put it… nice… so ladies, as my Mother told me when I was a child, make the most of every opportunity when it is presented to you!

And then we stopped at a shop selling cotton, for which of course Egypt is famous – I suspect it's a favourite stop for all the guides. We had been warned about the party night – (I still shudder at the very memory!) when we would all be expected to dress up in Egyptian clothes and, although we weren't told it at this stage, make fools of ourselves. We each bought a *galebeah*, dark navy for David, who at over 6'2" looked wonderful and the large white trainer shoes somehow added to the overall picture. John's was green with short sleeves and mine shocking pink with long sleeves. Himself chose a rather pale looking one which I felt made him look very anaemic, but he liked it. Purchases made, and we all jumped back onto the coach for a short ride to the Temple of Luxor, almost opposite where the *m.s. RA* was moored.

THE TEMPLE OF LUXOR was very different to the others – none of the 'estate built houses' for the ancient Egyptians – so many different ideas on a theme, and no two temples alike. A graceful temple, which overlooks the Nile, Luxor was once linked by the avenue of sphinxes with the temple of Karnak. Built of sandstone, it covers 4 acres, which is minute compared to Karnak, but it has a much more gentle kind of beauty. As with the other temples, we saw a mass of hieroglyphics, wonderful statues, fantastic columns and another obelisk.

The boat was calling and waiting for us, as we boarded by walking across several gangplanks, was another delicious lunch followed by a quiet afternoon watching the banks of the Nile pass by on our way upstream to Esna lock and the Temple of Esna.

Sitting on the sun deck we watched scenes from the Bible. Just when you think you've seen it all, around the next bend in the river is a delicate minaret, tall and slender, rising above the mud houses and palm trees. The next bend reveals a wonderful mud brick temple or fort, straight out of Lawrence of Arabia – should that be Lawrence of Egypt? Then more mud brick houses, children, who can have absolutely no idea what life is like on board this boat, waving from the banks, fishermen in their tiny boats, tatty-sailed feluccas – long narrow boats with very tall thin sails – water buffalo and beautiful white birds which I believe were Ibis.

"So what's this A.B.C.?" I asked David and John as they sat beside me wrapped in towels, trying to get warm following their plunge into the icy swimming pool.

"What?" they said in unison, looking at each other a little guiltily.

"Come on now. Every morning it's the same. The xylophone goes and you both yell 'Not A.B.C., not A.B.T.'"

They giggled.

"Not another bloody camel Mum," said John with a grin.

"And therefore, not another bloody temple," added David.

I could see their point. We had seen plenty of both.

We lazed around on the top deck, warm in the sunshine, absorbing the atmosphere, but too afraid we might miss something to allow sleep to take over. We were making for the lock at Esna, where we were warned we would probably be in a queue of boats to go through, and unfortunately we probably would go through the lock when we were all asleep. Since the advent of the two dams at Aswan, the amount of water in the Nile has been altered, and it no longer floods each year. Equally, it takes a long time for the lock to fill between boats.

The sun sank to a perfect sunset – just what the tour company and the film makers ordered. The desert, the Nile, palm trees, camels and the slowly sinking sun.

Tied up in the queue for the Esna lock, we were surrounded by little boats each with a couple of local merchants, all desperate to sell their goods. From the top deck of our boat we shouted down to them – I really didn't want the *galebeah* they held up, but the fun of bargaining, the ridiculously low price of the black caftan-type dress with *rare, exotic pearls and gold sequins* kept us entertained for nearly an hour. I ended up buying it for five Egyptian pounds and five English pounds, a total of just under £6 sterling. It'll probably fall apart when I do get around to washing it: there were at least another six in the dining room that evening, all with the same *rare, exotic pearls and gold sequins* but never before have I bargained for and bought goods whilst standing five floors up above a tiny rowing boat! The merchants were excellent at throwing the goods up onto the top deck! Occasionally something ended up in the water, but not often, and invariably that had been thrown down by a passenger – obviously he didn't play cricket for England.

ESNA – TEMPLE OF KHNUM, the ram-headed creator – a square temple that appears to be built in a huge pit. In fact the level of the ground around it has risen so high that the temple roof is now level with the foundations of the nearby houses. The temple is almost entirely unexcavated with much still buried under the surrounding houses. All we could see was the first hypostyle hall with its pillars. The pillars in this temple are wonderful, each with a different top, or capital. We walked from the ship to the temple, the last couple of hundred yards being through the local 'Oxford Street'.

"If you felt pressurised by the local salesmen before," Tarek warned us as we left the boat, "you haven't seen anything yet!"

And he was right. Even John, by now our champion bargain hunter, wasn't interested in shopping in this place, and got through the street as quickly as he could, returning to the boat for lunch whilst the banks of the Nile slipped past.

EDFU – TEMPLE OF HORUS – son of Osiris who, if you remember was murdered and dismembered. You need to know these things! You never know when a question will crop up in the Syndicate Quiz on board *Aurora*!

This is the best-preserved temple in Egypt with the construction of the newer temple having been started in 237BC and completed around 57BC – a temple dating back to the Old Kingdom was recently discovered underneath. We rode to the temple in a horse drawn buggy, John being allowed to join the driver on top! In the temple are two statues of falcons in black granite and also a replica of the sacred barque (boat) used for the procession of the gods. Again, the hieroglyphics were absolutely wonderful.

The pace of this cruise is quite intense, and we began to appreciate another relaxing afternoon watching the riverbanks as we sailed on towards Kom Ombo.

That evening was the party night and I'm still cringing at the thought! The early part was a superb buffet dinner with many Egyptian foods as well as European. Because we were in the week immediately prior to Christmas, by now the decorations were out, including a Christmas tree. All of which felt rather strange in the temperatures we were enjoying.

After supper we all went to the bar, wearing our *galebeah*, yashmaks etc. Luckily I had persuaded Himself to buy another *galebeah*, this one being black with a black and gold jacket, and on his head he wore a fez, and looked very handsome. A bath towel and some charcoal to make a beard, turned him into a high priest for the play in which he had to perform. He certainly looked the part. I was chosen to play a woman out shopping with friends (how had Tarek picked up on my favourite hobby?) and pretend to be bargaining in the local market. I hated drama at school with a vengeance, and I can only say my dislike has not lessened over the years. But it was to get worse.

As we entered the bar, we had each been given a ticket. A raffle, we wondered? But no! Each of us in turn had to stand and dance to the local music, egged on by the band and staff. Dreadful embarrassment for many people! There were those amongst us who retired to their cabins for a rather extended *visit* – in retrospect maybe Himself was right. John and David got up and did a very passable example of a sand dance to the applause of the audience. I doubt I'd have had the guts to do it at their ages.

Then it was my turn, so I ignored my number as it was called. The eyes of the entire audience were upon me and my embarrassment. The number was called again and thankfully Tarek got up and joined me, slightly lessening the embarrassment and tying the scarf around my then slender hips to the cheering of the band.

Not only did I hate drama at school, I am also tone deaf and possess little sense of rhythm… I prefer to gloss over the next *long* five minutes, but suffice it to say I was not at all surprised when I didn't win one of the prizes for the ten best dancers. Should I ever be lucky enough to go on another Nile cruise, I too will take the evening off and read a book peacefully out of sight!

KOM OMBO – a double temple devoted to the crocodile God Sobek and Horus the elder.

It was early morning when we walked off the ship after breakfast and strolled to the temple – at least I think it was. It was far too early after the previous night's festivities, and the sun did absolutely nothing for my hangover which had been gained by my efforts to drown my embarrassment. I don't remember a great deal about Kom Ombo except that I saw some mummified crocodiles, which are no longer able to reach this far north as their journey is now blocked by the Aswan Dam. At Kom Ombo there is also a very good Nilometer, which was used to measure the height of the Nile floods. Before the Aswan Dam, the Nile flooded each year and in the days of the temples, the people paid taxes depending on how high the floods were. Not high enough, low taxes as the crops wouldn't grow. High enough, high taxes as they had good crops. Too high, low taxes as everything was washed away! Now there's an idea instead of the Council Tax.

Several hangovers were now slowly, with relief, returned to the cool of the boat for the final cruise to Aswan.

Aswan is situated at the gates of what was once Lower Nubia, now taken over by the vast Lake Nasser, which was created by the damming of the Nile. It's a beautiful town and the most southerly stop for the Nile cruisers.

Just as I hear you all saying "Not A.B.T. coming up", there is, but it's our final A.B.T. and in some ways the most beautiful as it's on an island in the lake between the old dam which was built by the British, and the High Dam built by the Russians and Egyptians. When the old dam was built it was obvious that the **TEMPLE OF PHILAE** would disappear, as it would be submerged by the new lake, so with funds raised by UNESCO, the temple was removed, stone by stone, to the nearby higher island of Agilkia where it was rebuilt to resemble the original.

We boarded small boats to go over to the island. The great Temple of Isis is the principal building on the island. As with most of the temples we had seen, this temple was in fact several temples built at different times and to different gods. Beautifully preserved hieroglyphics and magnificent columns, and very difficult to see just what was original and what restored.

We left our last temple, although some of us were to go back later that evening for another Sound and Light – quite different to the one at Karnak – the approach in the dark in little boats being spectacular, if a little insecure.

Before returning to the ship, we visited the unfinished obelisk – can you imagine carving this huge obelisk measuring 137 feet in length and weighing some 1,168 tons, to have it split just as you were nearing the end? I don't know what the Egyptian is for "oh dear me", but I suspect it was said more than once!

The following morning arrived and with it our last full day before the journey home. We decided not to visit Abu Simbel as it involved an early start and an air flight, and was, according to David and John, just another bloody temple! Instead, the four of us wandered into Aswan town and strolled through the local market, the noise of the traders encouraging potential clients, people bargaining for lower prices, mixing in with the sound of cars and motorbikes, children shouting and playing games. More films were used. There was a wealth of sights to photograph, and a multitude of smells to remember, some not particularly pleasant ones... the men selling fish and scraping off their scales... men selling chickens and pigeons held captive in wooden crates, and a poor old turkey who looked at me sadly as if to say 'please don't buy me – I don't like Christmas'… endless stalls selling t-shirts with Egypt painted across them. Table linen, boxes made of camel bone or more expensive ones of mother of pearl. Hubble bubble pipes, *galebeah*, strong smelling spices, brilliantly coloured bloated tomatoes, oranges, a multitude of vegetables, fruits, camel meat with the odd camel head still on the chopping block, and the local version of pigs trotters – but this time camel trotters.

Ladies walking in their black gowns, a few wearing yashmaks, but nearly all carrying their shopping on their heads – maybe you could try it in Sainsbury's the next time you shop there. It was a noisy, happy crowd of mostly very friendly people. We did see a few beggars and also one poor man who I suspect had leprosy, but on the whole most people looked well clothed, happy and well fed.

Following our last floating lunch on *m.s. RA* we boarded a felucca for a sail to Kitchener's Island to see the botanical gardens. In the heat of the summer it must be a peaceful oasis of green – tree sized poinsettias, palms and other exotic plants. The island had been converted into a botanical garden by Lord Kitchener, and now into a public garden managed by the Ministry of Irrigation. Today it is full of rare and exotic plants from all over the world. It was here I wished we'd had longer to linger.

Back onto the felucca. No wind so we had to have a tow from a passing motorboat, which rather spoilt the ambiance! Whenever you see a picture of Aswan there are always these graceful feluccas and to be towed by a noisy motorboat full of young Egyptians obviously enjoying the situation, did nothing to add to the romance of where we were going.

On to the West Bank and a walk up to the Mausoleum

of the Aga Khan. The inner walls of the Mausoleum are marble. It was peaceful and cool inside and we had to remove our shoes before we could enter. Very simple, but very beautiful, the Aga Khan's wife, the Begum, had him buried here in February 1959 and thereafter each day had a rose placed on his sarcophagus. It's hard to imagine a more beautiful and romantic place to end your days. As I said to Himself, I hope he'll find somewhere like that for me, but not for a few years yet. She must have loved him very dearly, and in 1991 she still maintained a home within walking distance of the Mausoleum.

The walk to the top took about 20 minutes, but was well worth the effort as the view from the top was breathtaking across the Nile and Aswan. Just as we were leaving, we were given a real Lawrence of Egypt sight. A camel with rider was silhouetted against the sky on top of a sand dune. We returned to our felucca for a row back to the *m.s. RA* – still no wind – and our last evening on board, complete with belly dancer.

As Tarek said, "Once you've seen one belly dancer, you've seen 'em all!"

We knew what he meant, but John and David seemed to enjoy her. They both chose *ring-side seats*, with cameras at the ready, until the lady, having wobbled her way around the room a little at first, started to ask individuals from the audience to join her. I have never seen either David or John move quite so quickly into *safer* seats!

Packing was rather sad – we had Christmas to look forward to, but we'd all enjoyed a fantastic trip into history, and one I'd repeat tomorrow. It's a very comfortable way to see a very beautiful part of the world and when we visited it was without the normal crowds of tourists. The first Gulf War had stopped a lot of American tourists and until they returned, the Egyptians were relying on the British.

And yet the holiday wasn't really over. After breakfast the following morning and a sit on deck for the last time watching the hustle and bustle that is busy Aswan, we boarded our air-conditioned coaches for the long drive back to Luxor to catch our flight. Here we were driving along the edge of the desert and through small villages. We'd been provided with delicious lunch boxes by the ship and we munched our way merrily behind a pick-up truck carrying four camels, men riding donkeys, camels carrying sugar cane, children at the side of the road waving. Every so often we were given tantalising glimpses of buildings as we flashed past, wonderful views of the Nile and of Nile cruisers carrying yet more happy tourists to A.B.T. And all the time the wonderful sunshine which kept the temperature in the very comfortable low 20's for most of the week. The nights are cool which made sleeping very easy. I wouldn't want to do the trip in the late spring or summer, as to avoid the heat of the day it means 05.00 starts to get to the temples before they heat up.

A quick stop – how do they call it – a *comfort* stop… only this time it wasn't, comfortable or clean, in fact it was very crude and little more than a hole in the ground. At first we hesitated, but our packed lunch complete with bottle of water got the better of us, and first one lady and then another braved the *lack of facilities* in the comfort stop. Yuck! It brought to mind my mother's advice, "never turn down the offer of a clean loo". Aren't men lucky?

Back on to the coach with unwashed hands – what a relief it was to arrive at Luxor airport!

And so you're back where you started – of course in 1991 the four of us caught a flight back to London ready to celebrate Christmas, but you're jumping on my multi-coloured hand-made magic carpet and coming straight back to *Aurora*. Have a safe journey – have your Cruise Cards ready, and I'll see you on board.

9

FLORENCE & ROME

Well I knew it would happen, and I wasn't at all surprised when you missed the ship's departure from Livorno. I know how enticing and magical the River Nile can be. Expecting you to cram all those temples into one day was a bit much – even doing it in two days was pretty amazing. But I'm glad you're back now and hope you've enjoyed the experience.

I've lost count of how many times we've visited Florence, but this is the first time by coach from Livorno. Yes, we could have made our own way there by train, but as I said before, miss the return train and you miss the ship. Being collected by an air-conditioned coach at the bottom of the gangway is much more civilised, and certainly by the end of the day will be much appreciated rather than a train full of hot bodies.

The lady accompanying the coach spoke excellent English and during the one and a half hour's drive on smooth roads, she gave us a commentary as we went through the Tuscan countryside, past hills, vines and crops of every variety – cypress trees, olives and stone oaks in profusion. I knew that olive trees live for hundreds of years and are regarded by some to have spirits of their own, but did you know that when cut down, they will invariably regenerate?

Neither did I know why the famous Ponte Vecchio now only houses shops selling gold. Vasari's Corridor passes across the bridge over the tops of the shops and allowed Cosimo I to cross the river and reach the Pitti Palace without running the risk of being assassinated. Before the 16th Century some of the shops sold meat. Can you imagine what the pong was like that rose from the butchers' shops in the middle of the summer heat? The ruling families didn't like the smell as, unseen by the ordinary people, they crossed from one side of the river to the other, and I'm not surprised. So it was decreed that only gold could be sold in the shops that line both sides of the bridge. An absolute heaven for ladies! An absolute nightmare for the gentlemen!

We got off the coach and were taken by our guide along the Via de'Malcontenti, to the Piazza of Santa Croce.

"I know why it's called that," Himself sprang into action.

"After such a journey, we all need the loo. We're all *malcontents*!"

He was, of course, right. More than one pre-occupied face echoed his feelings!

Our guide pointed out a leather factory where we could all use the toilets. It came as no surprise to find we were faced with a long walk between rows and rows of handbags and leather jackets to the very rear of the shop where the toilets were situated!

Before casting us adrift – these nautical terms do take over even when on dry land – and allowing us free time until late afternoon, our guide pointed out our meeting place. The Basilica of Santa Croce is one of the largest churches in the city, and is partially surrounded by a flight of stone steps... now in brilliant, scorching sunshine, these steps by the afternoon, she promised, would be cool and in the shade and would provide plenty of seating for all of us!

"Around the next corner. He'll be there," Himself said, full of confidence in his map reading, and he was right.

"Ah David!" I sighed.

Poor David – this visit he was covered in scaffolding, but still a magnificent sight, even if he's only a replica of the real thing. On visiting Michelangelo's David in the Galleria Dell'Accademia on our first holiday in Florence, I wouldn't have been surprised if he had stepped down off his podium and walked towards me, so lifelike is the marble sculpture. Photographs and copies of the statue just don't convey that special something, the muscular power, those huge... *hands!*

We thoroughly enjoyed Florence, just the two of us, Himself and I, hand in hand, pottering as befits our age, revisiting old haunts and finding a couple of new ones too. Florence has some excellent leather outlets, and naturally we were caught, as if by magic, by a handbag shop, but then black and red is always in fashion and I'll enjoy the bag for many years to come... and every time I look at it, I'll have more happy memories of a very romantic city.

Lunch, pasta of course, was lingered over in a very Italian way sitting at an outside table in an eating-house, a mixture of pavement café and bistro – in the UK it would be considered to be in an alleyway, but the sunshine and the view of the Duomo upgraded this one to a desirable restaurant. We felt very Italian, sitting side by side and remained seated after we'd finished our pasta to enjoy some people watching, savouring the remains of our bottle of Barolo, gazing into each other's eyes, and at the same time enjoying the view of the magnificent Duomo only a hundred yards away.

There were one or two other people visiting Florence yesterday! That should read one or two hundred thousand people! The place was packed. My photographs, which I can have developed on board of course, show a sea of faces and acres of blue. Blue is obviously the colour preference for tourists' t-shirts this year regardless of the nationality of the wearer.

Little has changed since our last visit, except of course for the Euro. Life in Italy is much easier for the tourist now that we're not converting millions of Lira into the Sterling equivalent. Life in Italy is now much more expensive for the Italians.

There is, however, one very noticeable difference since our last visit, and here we're not talking Euros. I don't know how to put this delicately, but we're talking... to put no finer point on the subject (and please excuse *that* pun!)... private parts!

The sculptors and painters in the 15th and 16th centuries left little to the imagination – a biology class of ten year olds would have had a field day. Some *members* on the statues and paintings may be slightly over stated, but stated they are! It has always been so. No doubt you noticed it was the same yesterday with many of the hieroglyphics – the Egyptians were obviously prone to exaggeration too.

However the difference lies in the modern interpretations. This visit it was difficult to avoid willies! Willies here and willies there, willies on postcards, and willies on birthday cards – please don't send me one – willies on scarves and handbags: no I didn't get one on mine! There were willies on tea towels and tray cloths, willies on folders and writing pads and, of course, willies on endless t-shirts.

Having secured one of the few seats outside a little café overlooking the Basilica of Santa Croce and whilst we were having our large Italian mixed ice creams, pistachio, strawberry, amaretto and chocolate for me – yes I know I deserved to be sick – what did I have to endure, but a gynormous willy and accompanying it, how can I put it, *paraphernalia* on a plastic pinafore hanging from the side of the market stall next to the café. I watched as it all waved dizzily in the breeze.

And, to spoil totally the end of our visit, we were joined by four beach-towel bagging Germans. On a passenger list lacking in *von* this and *herr* that, there are few if any German passengers getting up at the crack of dawn and bagging all the best sun bathing positions on sun deck. This job is left to some of the English passengers, but at a more respectable hour, after breakfast.

Today in Piazza Santa Croce they arrived, took the two remaining unoccupied tables and proceeded to move them nearer to the edge of the pavement, determined that no-one should get between them and the passers by.

"Left their towels at home," Himself muttered, but softened slightly when one *herr* turned and talked to him about his choice of ice cream in a cultured English voice with very little hint of an accent.

And it wasn't all bad – the large German head hid David's private parts perfectly from my view, whilst I finished off my gargantuan ice cream.

* * * * *

But that was yesterday, and today, whilst you've been reading hieroglyphics, we visited a dear old friend of Himself, a retired Italian Admiral. Enzo and Himself met over 50 years ago on a train, when Himself was having problems with his Italian whilst in conversation with a ticket collector. Enzo, then a young naval officer, offered to help and explained in his basic English that in Italy you pay extra to travel on a train on a Bank Holiday... and they've remained friends ever since.

The young naval officer steadily climbed in seniority until he ended his career as Senior Admiral in Rome of the Italian Navy. Still a dashingly handsome man when I met him over 20 years ago, he must have been absolutely delicious as a young officer!

We have stayed several times with Enzo and Lia, his wife, in their villa north of Rome and were delighted when their daughter and granddaughter offered to collect us for the day. We had hoped to entertain them on board *Aurora*, as we were lucky enough to have been able to do on board Fred. Olsen's *Black Watch* in 2001 courtesy of Captain Drablos, but since 9-11, as everyone appears to refer to the dreadful Twin Towers disaster, any ship visits are totally out of the question. Life has changed in so many little ways since that awful day, as well as the major changes that we all know about.

It was such a pity. I remember Enzo being open mouthed at the equipment on the Bridge of the *Black Watch* – a ship built in 1972 but obviously updated since then. Since his days at sea, modern ships are now equipped with Satellite Navigation that tells the officers on the Bridge to a couple of feet where the ship is anywhere in the world, and equipment giving the exact depth beneath the keel! I had been amused that day to see a yellow Post-it® note stuck on the side of a screen saying 'Wake Steward'. Obviously even in the high-tech atmosphere of a modern ship's Bridge, that early morning cuppa is still important.

If, as he had been, Enzo was impressed by the bridge on the relatively small and somewhat aged *Black Watch*, imagine how he would have reacted to *Aurora's* Bridge. Gone are the days of the Captain and crew getting wet as they walk out onto the Bridge's open projection to the port or starboard with their binoculars around their necks. *Aurora's* Bridge is totally enclosed – all glass – very much state of the art. It's like comparing a Model T Ford to a Rolls Royce.

However, it was not to be. Apart from a polite explanation and refusal from Captain Walters, our old Admiral friend wasn't well enough to make the trip to Civitavecchia, so we went to him through the chaotic traffic that is Rome on the Pope's birthday – P&O wasn't to know when it arranged the itinerary for this cruise! In case you don't know where you are now, you've returned from your trip on the magic carpet, and we're just leaving Civitavecchia, the port for Rome.

Back to the Euro. Everyone we spoke to in Corsica, Italy, and later Spain, all complained that since the Euro the cost of living has risen alarmingly. Even our dear Admiral and his daughter who is a journalist but also works for the Italian government, said the same. Maybe we should take heed in the UK.

Mr and Mrs F.T.C. did it all – a full day in Florence and Pisa yesterday and a full day in Rome today.

"See what you mean about sea days," Mr F.T.C.

smiled as we met in Reception.

"Can't wait for the next one," Mrs F.T.C. agreed.

"Try a trip to Cape Town," I suggested. "You'll get plenty of sea days on the way there. The only trouble with Mediterranean cruises and modern shipping, is that all the ports are too close together. Or you could always join us on *Oceana* in September when we're going to Venice and Dubrovnik," I added.

Now, in case you're beginning to think this ship is a floating old peoples' home, I've just looked at tonight's programme, planned to ensure that we all have an *opulent* or a *perpetual* evening – and before you wonder – last night we enjoyed a *magnificent* or a *never-ending* evening – on board *Aurora*. Apart from a singer and a comedian in the Curzon Theatre, there is Karaoke in Champions' Bar. Are you in good voice? Could you be the next Elvis or Cliff? Why not give it a try? You might win a bottle of 'bubbly'. Or failing that, what about a comfortable seat in the Playhouse where at 22.15 Daniel Radcliffe and Emma Watson are appearing in *Harry Potter and the Chamber of Secrets?* Dancing in Carmen's, a quiet drink in the Crow's Nest, or if you've any brain cells left after your long trip to the Nile, how about joining a table in Vanderbilt's for the Syndicate Quiz? You never know, there may be a question on Egyptian temples. And in Masquerade's the Beat Goes On, from 23.00 until late! Somehow sore feet and tired bodies will probably mean that 'late' tonight isn't as late as usual.

* * * * *

I almost forgot. Are you happy with your table in the dining room? I should have asked you before. Your place at that table isn't written in stone, and it is possible to change to another table, although we've only had to do that once in all the years we've cruised.

When you book a cruise you are normally asked whether you'd like a table for two, four, six or eight – we have friends who always choose a table for two, but to me, part of the fun of cruising is meeting new people, and a table for six or eight increases the number of people you will get to know. A table for four can be a little difficult as you are only going to meet one other couple at dinner time, but the choice is yours.

On arrival on the ship you will normally find a card in your cabin giving dining room details, and we always make a point of visiting the dining room as soon as possible and just having a look at where we've been placed. Invariably it's absolutely fine, but just occasionally I know people have found they're on a table for four when they asked for eight, or eight when they wanted to sit alone. A request to the Manager of the dining room at this stage is often able to correct any problem.

There is also the unlikely situation when you'll be on a table where you feel totally at odds with every other person on that table. It is highly unlikely. On the whole people who cruise are a sociable lot and usually like to get to know their fellow shipmates. Again, you can always request to be moved.

If all else fails, and you'd prefer to eat elsewhere, on *Aurora* there is always the option of eating in Café Bordeaux where food is served 24 hours a day. Most modern cruise ships now have their own version of Café Bordeaux, which means you can of course avoid ever going into the dining room, but it would be a great pity.

And another thing I should have mentioned before, but you all seem to be a pretty healthy lot, what happens if you get sick on *Aurora*? Well, you go to see the doctor, just as you would do at home, only you won't have to wait so long for an appointment. Himself is on Warfarin, a blood-thinning drug – indeed several of the passengers will be – and he occasionally needs to check his blood clotting levels. It is always comforting to know that the medical facilities on board can cope with most problems we passengers will come up with. There is a team of doctors and nurses on board and two surgeries each day. Watch *Aurora Today* for times, as morning surgery is later on sea days to allow for passengers lying in and recovering from days in port. Of course emergencies are dealt with at any time of the day or night.

So Himself and I went down to the Medical Centre this morning, and sat in the waiting room. The hospital, for indeed that is what it is, has five wards, each with two or three beds, and has intensive care facilities. The doctors are able to do what they call minor procedures, but would hesitate to do much more unless it really was a matter of life and death. Even in mid-Atlantic they would rarely operate on an appendicitis, preferring to control the problem by drugs until land based hospital facilities are available.

Personally I find this all very comforting – think unsteady sea, think unsteady doctor's hand, see untidy scar!

"Hi," I said to a cheerful looking lady in a wheel chair whilst Himself was having his blood test.

"You've obviously got plastered," I added, indicating the large cast on her leg. "Have you been line dancing?"

"As if! Fell off a pavement!" she laughed.

"Should have added more tonic in it," I replied.

"Husband trying to get me away from the jewellery shops on the Ponte Vecchio!"

"He pushed you off the pavement?"

"No – I was looking backwards at the bracelet I liked whilst walking forwards!"

"Done much damage?"

"Two broken bones in the foot. The tour guide was absolutely brilliant, but the Italian hospital was deadly!"

We laughed.

"We just don't know how lucky we are in England with the NHS," she carried on.

"They X-rayed it eventually, but couldn't plaster it as it was too swollen. They did this on board," she indicated the plaster from toes to knee.

"I'm back for a little trim," she added, pointing to the overhang at the base of the plaster.

"They've been wonderful here. Provided a wheel-chair and crutches," she added.

"Muscle control – I've got very good muscle control," Plastered of Worcester went on. "Going to lose it all now. I have to keep my foot off the ground for six weeks."

"Will they let you take the wheelchair home on loan?" I asked.

"Bit difficult in the motorway café if they don't," she said. "We have to go to Worcester, and I'm not a camel although I will resemble a zebra when they take the plaster off – half one leg will be white, and the rest brown."

She was still laughing when we parted. I somehow don't think she and her plaster will be abandoned on the quayside at Southampton.

There are indeed splendid medical facilities on board, and somewhat different to our Banana Boat trip some years ago where the Captain was supposed to act as doctor and cope with anything!

Good the facilities are, but they get better. The doctors on *Aurora* have the facility of seeking advice from a shore-based consultant via satellite. An x-ray taken on board can be sent via satellite to the consultant who can then talk to the doctors on board. Sort of gives you confidence, doesn't it?

Anyway, it's nearly midnight and we've all had a long day and there's another port in the morning. Hope you've enjoyed your *opulent* or *perpetual* evening on board the good ship *Aurora*. See you in the morning.

10

DAYS OF BEAUTY, DEHYDRATION AND SPOTS

Already it's Monday and we're over half way through our fortnight's cruise and here we are at anchor in the Bay off the famous French resort of Cannes.

Of course normally there is a lot to see and do on shore, but we are here at Film Festival time and also the rally drivers and officials are preparing for the Monte Carlo Rally. So today the whole area will be packed, just like a can of sardines. Most of the passengers are rushing ashore, some to visit Monaco and drive around the rally route, some to outlying resorts to escape the crowds, but the great majority just to mooch, shop and people watch in Cannes. Terry and Jean are doing this – will the Jack Nicholson look-alike be mobbed and asked for his autograph, or will he perhaps come face to face with his famous double?

It's about now that you realise why I prefer sea days. We've had four consecutive days in port – unless of course you've been up the Nile – and tomorrow will be the fifth. Seasoned cruisers learn to pace themselves – first time cruisers try to do everything and often disembark at Southampton in need of another holiday.

In the past we've driven along the Golden Corniche and enjoyed the beautiful scenery, strolled around Cannes and visited Nice. Been there, done that, and got the t-shirt, as the saying goes. This is one of the joys of cruising, in that we don't feel the need to abandon ship every time she heads for port, and we are able to enjoy the facilities on board of what then feels like a private yacht, as *Aurora* has felt today, devoid of most of her passengers. Our tenders have been providing a continuous ferry service to take eager passengers to Cannes, sweltering in the sunshine about a mile from the ship, and then bringing back exhausted passengers who have spent time ashore. It has been utterly exhausting watching all the to-ing and fro-ing.

* * * * *

Skin type – dehydrated. The words shout at me from the page. Dehydration! A sin. Not enough water. Too much wine. Too much sun. Anyone would think I was on holiday!

I'm in the Beauty Salon and I've been cleansed and toned and plastered with seaweed gunk, covered in a fabric mask, and, unable to see, left lying alone to cook like a beached whale, left with nothing to do but relax, a tape of the sounds of seagulls and waves dulling my senses and removing any resistance which remains following the wine enjoyed during our elongated lunchtime.

Sophie returns. A pretty young girl who has done

almost a whole year working in the Beauty Salons on ships.

"Are you enjoying it?" I ask what I think is a safe question.

"Not really. I'm bored by all the partying and the endless travel."

She says she won't be returning following her completion of this contract. I wonder at her sanity! How could anyone be tired of life on board? But, of course, passenger life is obviously very different to life below stairs.

"…not much salary," she continues as she removes all the lotions from my face.

"…very few tips this cruise," she adds. I make a mental note!

"…skin's very good for your age, but it's dehydrated."

Her words snap me back to the present.

And then the hard sell starts.

"… *special offer… only £50… wonderful value… cures dehydration… encourages youthful skin… protects… prevents dehydration… special offer… wonderful value… it's up to you… it's up to you… special… youthful…*"

Why is it when you're horizontal, mentally reduced to the level of an overripe melon, partially asleep and at your most vulnerable, feeling wonderfully relaxed, the therapist has to go and spoil it all with the inevitable sales talk, having first turned down the sounds of the recorded seagulls and waves so that you won't miss a single, valuable word?

Today I found the perfect answer. Be strong and say calmly, but firmly, "I'll consider it tomorrow when I've seen how my skin reacts to your products," smile, give her a generous tip and make your way to the exit – speedily.

However, on this occasion, I don't escape without leaving her with the last word!

"The offer will only be available while stocks last!"

"Thank you Sophie," I smile. "I'll obviously have to take that risk."

"And don't forget to drink plenty of water tonight," she finishes as she hands me my prescription upon which she has written in bold letters, 'Skin Type – Dehydrated'!

It is, however, worth remembering that on port days the Beauty Salon on board often offers special reductions – today there was 20% off every treatment – but make sure you book early in the cruise as these offers are very popular.

Most cruise ships have a Beauty Salon on board, the size of which varies of course as does the extent of services offered. Men and women are catered for at prices similar to those on shore. The best hairdresser I ever met anywhere was on board a ship some cruises ago.

"I love that colour," he said – I'll call him Nigel – pointing to my evening outfit. One of the joys of going to a hairdresser on board is that you can attend in almost any form of dress. I've seen everything from dressing gowns and swimwear to gym outfits and full evening dress.

"It's absolutely lovely, quite lovely my dear," he went on, his firm strong hands shampooing my hair. "In fact I've always loved it. I even had some trousers made in just that colour in Hong Kong on the world cruise." He was working in the conditioner.

I blinked at the thought, trying to picture the bottom half of his 6'2" slim body swathed in fuchsia pink.

"Ordered them one day my dear, and they were ready to collect the next. Really amazing."

"Really," I said, somewhat lost for words, as he finished rinsing my hair.

"Must make sure I don't eat too much or they just won't fit," he added, wrapping a towel around my head. "They're just a teeny little touch too tight you know." He wriggled his hips. "But I still love them."

Nigel had joined this ship the day we started the cruise and was fairly new to cruising. Frequent cruisers get to know the hairdressers on P&O, Cunard and Fred. Olsen, all of whom are employed by land based companies, and are allocated to a ship for a contract period. When they return home at the end of their contract, they can then be placed on any other ship after their holiday. It must be a wonderful life if you're single and without responsibilities.

Throughout the duration of the cruise I visited Nigel frequently – a mature man in his late 50s who had recently lost his partner in an accident, he didn't fit into the usual type of hairdresser on board, and although I have seen plenty of men doing the job, they tend to be younger. I think to start with the young female beauticians and hairdressers gave him a hard time, moving his equipment and borrowing his brushes, but his gentle manner and calm attitude in face of pandemonium on a formal night when hairdressing salons become very busy, soon won them over. He did more than his share of work, always calm and unflappable, a stream of very satisfied ladies leaving his chair.

At the start I found him by accident, having gone to make an appointment.

"18.30 tonight my dear? Of course we can squeeeeeeeeeze you in. In fact I'll do it for you myself," he added, raising his beautifully sculptured eyebrows.

And so began three weeks of heaven, until I came to settle the large account at the end of the cruise, where every third item appeared to be hairdressing. Hairdressers at home are infrequent stops in my busy life. Here on board ship I have all the time in the world.

To begin with he was able to fit me in easily – the girls were always busy – he was the newcomer, his gentle lilting voice disguising his long, strong fingers, clever brush-ability and artistic scissors.

"Who did your hair?" How many times was I asked? I told too many people, and steadily his clients increased until it became almost impossible to book an appointment with him.

"What a beautiful sunset," I said on my last time in his chair as we were on yet another calm crossing of the Bay of Biscay on our way home.

"Doesn't it make you feel happy to be alive?"

"You know my dear, you're just like my mother! That's just what she would have said."

I smiled – he and I were much of an age, and I knew no insult was intended.

"I normally have her here with me," he added.

I let that sink in. I knew from our many previous conversations that she was dead, in fact had been dead for several years.

"But she's still in my cabin."

Had the heat on the long sea days finally got to him?

"I must bring her up here."

The look on my face made him smile, and gently nudging my shoulder with his brush holding hand, he added.

"There I go again. Her ashes my dear… her ashes. I've scattered most of them where she and I agreed before she died, but I kept just a bit of her, in a pretty little eye-cream pot, and she normally sits on there," he said pointing to the narrow shelf between me and the window through which the sun was slowly setting.

"You see I couldn't bear to part with her totally. There she can share the wonderful scenery and can be part of lovely conversations with people like you," he added with another nudge on my shoulder.

"Haven't decided if I like this ship or not," he went on. "Not decided if I'm going to stay or not," he added. "Won't bring her up here until I'm sure, but she'd have liked you.

* * * * *

Some time later, sitting on our balcony reading through a pile of bumf I had ignored when we boarded over a week ago, I announced to Himself in amazement.

"It's a theme cruise!"

"I know," he said wearily. "You obviously weren't listening when I told you."

Some cruises are designated 'theme cruises' and I should have told you all this before, but as you've probably already gathered, life on board ship can be very busy, and this cruise has been no exception. We're on a Classical Music theme cruise, and we have a wonderful collection of singers and musicians to entertain us for the whole fortnight, all introduced by our Musical Host, Richard Baker OBE, who seems to have changed little since I first saw him reading the news on television – is this a sign of old age? Mine of course, not his.

Whilst on the subject of theme cruises, if Classical Music isn't your choice, there is still plenty to do on board and you could be forgiven for not knowing that this is a Classical Music cruise if you have chosen to avoid all the concerts. There are many other theme cruises, which are indicated in the Cruise Line brochures. Antiques, Comedy, Soap Opera, Golf, Football, Fashion, to name a few – something for everyone. As with this cruise, if the theme isn't your scene, just ignore it, but if you do enjoy the theme, it will add something extra to your enjoyment of the cruise. Also when you book, don't forget to mention if you're a newcomer to cruising, or celebrating a birthday or wedding anniversary on board, or if you're on your honeymoon. Special packages are available on certain cruises, and why miss out on champagne and other goodies?

Cruising is the most wonderful way of getting to know famous performers from all fields of entertainment. In the past I've seen Angela Rippon's famous legs, discussed writing with Leslie Thomas and Mavis Cheek, and heard Pam Ayres' new poem called *Aurora*, which she wrote whilst on board *Aurora*. I've laughed at an endless list of comedians until my jaws ached and listened in amazement to the incredible playing of Nicola Loud a wonderful young violinist who won the Young Musician of the Year when only 15. The list of stars afloat goes on and on – lecturers, historians, artists, photographers.

All cruises on passenger ships have entertainment programmes and, whilst the performances are without exception as professional as they would be ashore, at sea there is the additional enjoyment of being able to mix with the entertainers around the ship when they revert to being like you and me, just passengers. Want to share a table at lunch with a singer? Play shuffleboard against a dancer, laugh at a comedian's natural humour by the side of the pool? Why not? We're all in this boat together, and by the end of the fortnight many new friendships will have been formed.

And if you sail with this Captain, don't be at all surprised to find him standing by your table in the Orangery where the lunch is self-service, and hear him ask, "Do you mind if I join you?" Captain Ian Walters is extremely friendly, and enjoys talking with his passengers. He's an interesting, amusing man who actually welcomes questions on anything to do with the sea and his ship – and motor racing, which is a hobby of his! But he's not alone and almost without exception the Captain and Officers on all the ships I have sailed on have been friendly and very approachable.

As usual in this area of the Mediterranean the calm seas of this morning are now becoming choppy. The crew will have fun securing the tenders before the Captain can announce, "All my ducklings are back on board and we are now setting sail for Barcelona."

* * * * *

"What? Nothing!" Mr F.T.C. says with surprise as we meet in the dining room for dinner at 20.30 at the start of our *riotous* evening on board – I was enjoying my facial when the passengers enjoying a *quintessential* evening were called to dinner.

"No. Absolutely nothing!" I smile.

"You stayed on the ship all day," he adds with a touch of envy.

My relaxed smile broadens as I nod my agreement.

"We thought we'd have a sea day," I add.

Here at anchor about a mile off Cannes it has been a beautiful, peaceful day, far removed from the chaos on shore.

"You didn't go people watching?" asks Mrs F.T.C.

"Nope! We spent most of the day relaxing on the balcony. Himself had a back massage in the early afternoon and I enjoyed a facial later on."

"Little wonder you look so relaxed," Mrs F.T.C. says with obvious envy, no doubt regretting their decision to rush around Monte Carlo instead of enjoying a day on *Aurora* which today resembled the *Marie Celeste.*

I must have been psychic when I said to Sophie I'd see how the products reacted on my skin. Half way through dinner it started, a tightening of the skin, an itch here, an unusual feeling there. The facial obviously did not agree with me. Now you rarely get to my age without experiencing the delights of a facial, of which there are many types available. I have my favourite, but today the beautician who could have given me that one was on shore leave in Cannes. The choice was simple. No facial, or sample the benefits of another with another beautician. You already know what decision I made! By the time I went to bed I was blotchy and by the following morning positively uncomfortable.

The doctor was sympathetic but declined my request to have something to remove the heat and stop the irritation.

"Keep out of the sun," he said, which is great news on a cruise.

"No lotions or creams and take one of these tablets each day with food – for three days!"

"Three days," I gasped. "I have to resemble a teenage acne sufferer for three days?"

It was just as well I could see the funny side of it all. Maybe next trip, I'll go on shore and sample the delights of Cannes!

11

VARIATIONS ON A THEME

*Time for some more poetic licence – and
I have a wonderful surprise for you all.*

As I said at the start of the last chapter, we are already over half way through our cruise. It's a well-known phenomenon that the second week of a cruise seems to pass at almost twice the speed of the first. I doubt there is a mathematical formula to explain this, but it does happen.

So! Do you really want to go back home already? Barcelona and Praia de Rocha and another crossing of the Bay are what's left of this cruise! Let's turn it into a magical mystery tour and take you off in totally the opposite direction. It means we'll have temporarily to jump ship, but with the twitch of my nose and a quick wave of my magic wand, and hey presto, we've joined another ship and gone back to 1994. Don't worry about your suitcases – poetic licence will take care of those, but do make sure you've packed your evening dress, as every night on board this ship is formal with a capital F… and I promise you won't miss out on visiting Barcelona as we will rejoin *Aurora.*

This one is not just *another* ship – she's something special and in 1994 she was a very special ship, luxurious and much more like a private yacht. Today in 2005 she's called *SeaDream I* and is owned by SeaDream Yacht Club, but in 1994 she was the pride of Cunard and called *Sea Goddess I.* The more you learn about cruising the more you'll realise that ships you pass today may well have been called something quite different when they were sailing for their previous owners. The Berlitz Ocean Cruising guide gives vast amounts of information about the different ships afloat, and is well worth purchasing if you get addicted to holidays afloat.

"Would you like to go on the cruise?" Himself asked as I was tidying up the kitchen. Not the sort of question he normally asked.

"Would I like to go on the cruise? Of course I jolly well would!"

But to set the scene…

Friends Michelle and Michael had booked a wonderful cruise on the *Sea Goddess I* back in March 1994 and naturally enough Himself and I were both very envious. We were new to cruising in those days, but we knew the words *Sea Goddess* meant all-inclusive luxury – wall-to-wall Champagne and caviar. Michael knew he had a major medical problem and had organised with Cunard at the time of booking, that should he be too ill to travel, Michelle could take a friend along instead – moi! An unusual arrangement, but one that Cunard had obviously agreed to as this gentleman was terminally ill.

As the departure date approached, Michael really

wasn't well and asked me to be ready to drop everything at the last minute. So I cleared the diary – moving the dental appointment was a real hardship – organised the house, filled up the cat food cupboard, prepared myself for a 'go/no go' situation, and tried to carry on life as normal, mentally already halfway through my first bottle of bubbly.

On the Tuesday evening Michael announced he felt a little better, and that no matter what, he would go with Michelle on the cruise. I was honestly delighted for them both, but understandably, of course, I was also somewhat disappointed. The following morning Himself made some secret phone calls, was told there was still availability on the cruise but that he'd have to arrange our flights himself. He checked that Michael and Michelle wouldn't mind us joining them, and then, finally, approached me.

"Yes please!" is the brief summary of what I actually said, and condenses the shrieks of delight and tears of joy.

"But I've got nothing to wear!"

"Then we won't go," Himself grinned.

"Oh I expect I'll find something!"

What a panic, but we did it, and Saturday morning found us at Gatwick with a problem over the airline seats.

"I can't sit by myself," I told the puzzled check-in girl as I turned from a mature 36 year old into a frightened child.

"Isn't there any way we can get two seats together?" Himself pleaded, holding my hand.

"I'm afraid we've only single seats left," the check-in girl repeated.

"Then I won't fly," I said, close to tears.

At which point Himself quietly explained that this was my first flight since the loss of my first husband in an air crash.

The exasperation of the queue behind us immediately turned to understanding.

"Just wait a moment, please," the check-in girl smiled at us, and disappeared to have a conversation with her boss.

Which is how our luxury cruise started by us being upgraded on the British Airways flight to Nice. Club Class was very peaceful and, a couple of glasses of Champagne later, life seemed very relaxed and I felt confident enough to allow the blood to return to Himself's hand. What a pity Nice wasn't half way around the world! Not only that, but several of the crew were ex-Dan Air employees and had known my late husband, a Dan Air pilot, so not only did we have superb attention, I was also given a couple of bottles of Champagne to *help me settle into my holiday better...* I didn't have the heart to tell the stewardess that Himself and I were going to be living on a floating cocktail cabinet for the next seven days!

At Nice airport, there was no representative from Cunard! We looked around for almost half an hour and then decided to grab a taxi and go to Monaco, where, we had been told, the *Sea Goddess I* was waiting for us.

"Parlez vous Anglais monsieur?" we tried on the very charming taxi driver, but he didn't. Have you noticed that virtually anywhere in the world the reply would have been 'a little' and a helpful smile, but not in France.

"Non" was all we received.

'Bateaux' and 'Monaco' got our message across and almost an hour later, even using the motorway, we arrived to find everywhere in chaos. That weekend was the Grand Prix, and emerging from one of the tunnels we found ourselves right next to the Williams Renault pit and crowds of people. (So now you see why we didn't feel the need to repeat the experience in Cannes yesterday!).

Eventually we found the Harbour Master's office, and Himself and the taxi driver left me sitting in the now very hot Mercedes, watching the life walk by. Skirts! They were at least the size of belts! Jewellery!… and that was not only on the ladies! If it hadn't been so hot, and by now we were both more than a little concerned as to where the ship was, it would have been a very amusing half hour. Tied up next to the taxi were millions of Pounds' worth of boats from all over the world. M'dears, if you must go to the Grand Prix, there is only one way to do it – go by boat and tie up next to the cliff on top of which is the Royal Palace.

"The *Sea Goddess* is in Nice!" Himself said as he got back into the taxi.

So we drove all the way back, at Cunard's expense, to Nice, where, sure enough this beautiful ship was tied up waiting for her last remaining passengers – us! Brief formalities on the quayside and we were on board, shaking the hand of the Captain and being given our first glass of Champagne, the first of many. Would it be *awfully* basic at this point to say I'd have loved a cup of tea? Probably, so I won't!

Having said "Hi!" to Michelle and Michael in their cabin – sorry, let's get this straight from the start, we are now on a luxury ship and they don't do cabins – no, we have suites. So, having said "Hi" to them in the suite next to ours, we quickly unpacked to return to the deck for cocktails as the ship left Nice at the start of the cruise. A gin and tonic later, another appeared – they had some very heavy-handed bar tenders! We wobbled our way back to the suite to change for dinner. A weak gin and tonic in the bar prior to dinner, plenty of white and red wine during dinner, and a brandy, or was it two, and it's little wonder I slept like a log – but I couldn't work out why the bed seemed to be moving – and it wasn't only the waves – next morning the results were obvious – I was hung over, and how!

At this point, in an effort to sober up, I'll describe the ship. She's a small ship of only 4,260 tons – compare that with *Aurora's* 76,000+ tons and you'll see why she felt like a private yacht. Normally when full, she could carry 116 passengers in 58 beautiful suites. Each suite can be used as either a double or two singles and each contained a sitting area with table which could be converted into a supper table should you wish to eat in the suite. Obviously there was an en-suite bathroom and also a safe, bar and fridge, television and video player, hairdryer etc etc etc. All food and drink on board was complimentary – including the five bottles of spirits and endless cans of mixers in the suite. The only bottles we got around to opening were the water bottles! No, we didn't go teetotal. We just had so much alcohol elsewhere on the ship, that we designated our suite an *alcohol free zone!*

(Having recently read the *Berlitz Ocean Cruising guide*, I see that some of the suites have been combined making larger accommodation, the sitting room being reached through an interconnecting door, and she now only carries 108 passengers with a crew of 89).

Facilities on the ship were extensive, from the swimming pool, which was apparently quite cold (even though it was May) to the gym, where not a lot of effort was used by our party. Breakfast and luncheon could be enjoyed in the main dining room or on deck if the weather was good. Afternoon tea was in the piano bar and dinner anytime from 20.00 either in the dining room or in our suite. In between times, should we feel hungry, Room Service would, of course, be able to supply anything from Champagne and caviar to a boiled egg, but I doubt there were many requests for the latter. At any time of the day or night all you had to do was ask for whatever you fancied, be it coffee or tea, iced cocktails, water, gin and tonic or even hot chocolate, as we found late one evening when we'd all had sufficient to drink and felt like a night-cap!

The passengers were mostly American – as always apparently – with some British, quite a number of Norwegians (it was their National Day whilst we were on board, and the crew were mostly from Norway – they were a cheerful lot!) and two from Nigeria, who hardly ever appeared from their room where, he assured me, he and his wife spent their time – talking!

As I said, the 'Officer' crew were mostly from Norway, the doctor, and I can still hear Michelle sighing about him, was tall, and grey, a retired surgeon and from Sweden. The waiters were French and German and the Maitre d' was from Scotland – he ran a 'tight ship' on the catering front – which is how we felt most of the time we were on board!

Are you bored by the experience or would you like to hear about the *beach party* which was held on our sea day by the swimming pool – more poetic licence – where a waiter walked into the pool carrying a tray of caviar high above his shoulders so that a swimmer could enjoy some in the middle of her swim! Had we been in the Caribbean, he'd have waded into the calm sea to passengers floating in the water on air beds. A buffet lunch was served around the pool and Michelle and I were well supplied with Champagne by Jacques, our friendly French waiter – any donation of blood at this point would have come out clear and bubbly! We became afraid to put a half full glass down even for a second, as Jacques would appear instantly to refill it.

In fact, dear readers, the week passed far too quickly in a haze of cocktail parties, wonderful food and excellent company. Cunard spent more on caviar than on fuel for the week's cruise. The four of us had lots of laughs and many happy moments. From the early morning tea – just press nine on the telephone, but it doesn't work at home – to the chocolate on our bed at night, every day was full of memories.

We sailed each day in the late afternoon and arrived at the next port early morning in time for breakfast. During the day, lifeboat number three, our lifeboat in case of need, was there to ferry us back and forth from the *Sea Goddess I* to the harbour. When we came back on board there were two waiters in attendance, one to give us an iced wet towel to refresh our hands in case we had touched something positive beastly on shore, and the other with a cool drink which contained '*mostly fruit juice*' – I bet it did! I won't bore you with the 08.00 Wake Up Stretch on Deck six, because none of us attended, nor the Low Impact Aerobics at 17.00 which were just not low enough for us, and anyway, we were far too busy deciding which kind of tea to have in the Piano Bar, where a wonderful selection of savouries and cakes were just waiting to be eaten!

Somewhere during the cruise we visited Portofino, Porto Cervo in Sardinia, Sorrento, Taormina in Sicily, Nisos Idhra – known to us as Hydra – and finally we arrived in Piraeus, the harbour of Athens. At Portofino we went to the Hotel Splendido and sampled the Ligurian food and olive oil before walking down a narrow path back to the busy town, full of tourists. Porto Cervo was disappointing. The weather was grey. We were told that the resort had been acquired by the Aga Khan in the 1960s and along with some colleagues he'd turned it into a luxury playground for the rich. To us, somewhat out of season, it held little of interest, especially as the shops were closed. No wonder Himself was quite happy, and Michael was even more delighted when we rejoined him on the ship without any purchases!

Sorrento was just as busy and wonderful as when we last visited, and here, thankfully Michelle and I were able to shop very successfully.

The weather in Taormina was unsettled and regrettably we were unable to catch more than a fleeting glimpse of Etna, still with snow near the summit. Taormina is a very beautiful town clinging to the hillside, and it must have spectacular views when the sun in shining. As with all the places visited, Cunard had laid on transport from the harbour to the resort – this time up a steep road full of hairpin bends!

Hydra was exceedingly beautiful, but so busy. It was full of thousands of school children on a day trip from Athens and also the poor donkeys upset all of us. As there are no cars on the island, they are used to transport everything. They looked so weary, had no shade and carried such heavy loads.

Each trip on shore was interesting but the return on board to the peace and quiet of the ship was even better. I haven't described in detail the shore visits as the real delight was the actual ship and the superb service, delicious food, endless liquid refreshment and our every need catered for. Smoked salmon for breakfast for me each morning, a waiter to open my honey pot in case I tired myself out using energy which might be needed to lift a glass of Champagne later in the day – the total lack of anyone waiting around for a tip – this really was an all inclusive luxury cruise.

The *Sea Goddess I* certainly spoils you for future holidays – unless of course they are on the *Sea Goddess II*, her sister ship – now there's a thought!

Except, the only drawback I can think of is that when she was built in 1984 none of the suites had private balconies – she should have waited a couple of years by which time luxury cabins were equipped with such delights.

* * * * *

So here you are, stranded in Athens having left the *Sea Goddess*. Of course, in 1994 the four of us flew straight home to the UK as we were scheduled to do, but why don't you have a wander around Athens. Visit the Acropolis and maybe have something to eat in Plaka, whilst I see what I can arrange for you…

12

A LITTLE BIT OF CULTURE

So – what did you think of Athens? Was it hot enough for you? I hope you enjoyed the air-conditioned coach tour of the city I organised for you. It should have given you a good overview, especially from the hill near the Acropolis from where you'll have had a magnificent view of this most famous of the ruins in Athens. The Temple of Zeus, Hadrian's Arch, Olympic Stadium, the Presidential Guard wearing their flattering short white skirts – wonderful for showing off the legs gentlemen – and Lycabettus Hill, (Mt. Lycavitos) which I actually climbed some years ago, before I became wiser – and older.

Even though we've all been overfed on board all of our cruise ships, I hope you found just a little room for your typical Greek lunch in Plaka, the old part of the city. Although I'm sure you've all tasted moussaka in the UK and no doubt in many other countries too, moussaka eaten in a restaurant in Plaka and washed down with Retsina with a fabulous view of the Acropolis towering in front of you takes a lot of beating.

Whilst we enjoyed our *poetic licence cruise* on the *Sea Goddess*, *Aurora's* dependable crew left Cannes and, as usual, found their next destination. So now, please jump back onto my magic carpet for a short flight. Let's go find ourselves *Aurora*!

* * * * *

From our vantage point on Sun Deck – well you'd hardly expect a magic carpet to land in the middle of the accommodation decks, would you – you'll now see the wonderful city of Barcel-**Oh**-na spread out in front of you.

Have you noticed how some advertisements stick in your brain? For me, it's those creatures from outer space in the Smash advertisement – 'first they peel them, then they boil them, and then they smash them to pieces!' – maybe it's the resultant hysterical giggles I remember most. The same goes for Barcel-**Oh**-na. As soon as I see or hear the word, I immediately remember the catchy signature tune every time we watched the Olympic Games on television in 1992 – but can it really be that long ago?

Today we are indeed tied up next to the dockside just a short shuttle bus ride from the centre of the city. And for some, it's time for a bit of culture. Here in Barcelona there is the usual good selection of tours to suit every taste, and those of you going on one of the first four tours should quickly make your way to the Curzon Theatre, collect your coach sticker and join your group.

P&O produced a wonderful book this year entitled 'Mediterranean Shore Excursions April – January' and I hope it's going to be a permanent fixture. Inside, in alphabetical order, are all the possible ports of call on any P&O Mediterranean cruise during the period – some that even I have never visited before. I must have a word with Himself and correct that omission!

Turn to Pages 11-17 and you'll find Barcelona and all 13 excursions listed, most of which are available on this cruise. They give the title of the excursion at the top, the duration, cost per adult and cost per child, followed by some symbols indicating levels of activity, whether the trip is especially suitable for children, if a meal is included in the price, whether there is any shopping, or if there are good photographic opportunities etc. Also at the front of the book there is a page giving all the general information you need to know about P&O excursions. This book is sent to your home address some weeks before the cruise, giving you plenty of time to decide where you'd like to go. On board every cruise there is a Port Lecturer who will describe the ports and answer any questions you may have.

But in general, if you've not visited a place before, an initial tour like today's Tour A – Highlights of Barcelona – is an excellent idea and will give you a great introduction to a wonderful city. Your tour guide will tell you about Barcelona as the coach driver smoothly navigates you through the heart of the city, probably whetting your appetite for more than just a bowl of paella. The tour lasts four hours and as we don't leave Barcelona until 17.30 this afternoon, you'll still have plenty of time to explore somewhere in more detail before catching the shuttle bus back to *Aurora*. And this is where the bit of culture comes in.

To students of Art, Barcelona is, of course, famous for one man, Gaudí. Everywhere you go you see balconies he designed on houses in the city, and, nowadays, endless postcards and books about his, to me, somewhat strange architecture. You can visit Gaudí's Church of La Sagrada Familia, designed in 1881 but never completed, although work has now restarted on this amazing structure, or go and spend some time in Parc Güell full of his wonderful mosaics, but take some spare films as you'll doubtless need them. But Barcelona is not just Gaudí, it also has *Museu Picasso* and houses the 58 paintings which Picasso donated to the museum in 1968 – in fact my guidebook lists six museums, which will obviously mean you need another cruise stopping in this city! Despite the number of times I've visited, I still haven't seen Joan Miró's work, but then modern art isn't my scene! The joy of cruising is that whatever you are 'in to', you will doubtless be able to find something of interest in most ports.

The swimming pools on *Aurora* are wonderful, but by virtue of their position on board a ship, they can be a little restrictive for those who want a *real* swim. Tour G – Sitges and swim, has a short tour of Sitges, a seaside town favoured by wealthy Catalan families, and a guided walking tour through the narrow streets of the old town. But the rest of the morning can be spent shopping, or if you prefer it, on the beach and maybe having that long swim – but don't forget to take your beach towel.

Been there? Done that? Then how about making a visit to Montserrat, famous for the Black Madonna, a beautiful Romanesque carved statue of Our Lady from the twelfth century. Approximately 25 miles from Barcelona, the Benedictine Monastery of Montserrat occupies a sheltered spot nestling into the side of the mountain, from where you get magnificent views of the surrounding countryside far below. The mountain rises some 4,055 feet above sea level and the whole area offers a wealth of photo opportunities with chapels and hermits' caves.

The Catalan word Montserrat means serrated mountain, which hints at the spectacular scenery you'll see should you decide on this trip – and don't forget to visit the Pastry Shop which will stave off any hunger pangs before you're able to sample some more delights created by *Aurora's* 120 chefs.

Feeling more energetic than that? Then why not go on Tour H – Barcelona Bicycle Tour. This tour has the symbol 'A' for *activity* – or maybe 'A' for *avoid*, if you're a more mature, sedentary person like moi!

You have children with you, or you're young in body or heart? Then Tour I – Fantasy Island Waterpark – could be for you. A 45 minute coach ride each way, it still leaves you with five clear hours at the Waterpark, long enough for even the most lively to exhaust all their pent up energy! The word 'bored' will not come to mind during this tour.

And for the man in your life, or for you lady golfers, Tour M entitled Golf is a visit to Caldes Golf Club, 45 minutes away by coach.

Now – have I forgotten anyone? Of course, Himself and I who are taking the shuttle bus which drops us at the Columbus Monument at the bottom of La Rambla. According to Somerset Maugham "it's the most beautiful street in the world". Lined with plane trees, the wide promenade up the centre between the two roadways is full of cafés, kiosks, flower sellers, newspaper vendors, seats and lots of people, all strolling in the shade in the heart of the old city.

Look out for the 'statues', apparently set in stone until one suddenly moves. Throw a coin into their collecting box and be rewarded with a clockwork-type bow, or just have a long, cold drink and watch the world go by.

The shuttle buses run regularly throughout the day and the time of the last shuttle back to the ship is always given in *Aurora Today*. Today's leaves the Colombus Monument at 16.30 and everyone should be back on board by 17.00 regardless of their mode of transport.

P&O also gives each passenger a Port Guide of each port visited, and this contains lots of information about where to visit within the city and beyond, methods of transport in the area, and telephone numbers of some restaurants – they obviously don't think we've eaten enough on board. It also advises as to the best buys shopping-wise and gives telephone numbers in case of emergency. There is a map on the back although often one is given to you on the quayside by the local tourist representatives as you step onto Spanish soil.

Too exhausted to do anything? Visiting five ports in five days (disregarding our two extra *poetic licence cruises*) is hard work and if you're just too tired to do anything, you can always stay on board and relax, although we do have a day at sea tomorrow and it would seem a pity to miss this wonderful city.

On board *Aurora* all the normal facilities are still available, except the shops and photo gallery which remain closed until we sail, as does the casino. Deck quoits, shuffleboard, bridge, whist and table tennis are still available, as is the library. The launderette should be quiet today and you won't have to queue for a machine. Of course, all the restaurants will be open, so starvation will not be a problem.

So why not find an empty sun bed, and enjoy the cocktail of the day, a 'Caribbean Sunset' made of Peach Schnapps, Malibu, pineapple juice and Grenadine.

Possibly follow that with today's speciality coffee, a 'Monte Cristo' made with Grand Marnier and Kahlua, let your eyes become heavy, your book rest on your increasingly comfortable stomach, and slowly fall asleep in the shade on a virtually empty Sun Deck.

* * * * *

Wake up! We're back, complete with an El Corte Inglés carrier bag. This is one of the well-known department stores at the top of La Rambla, and unlike many Spanish shops, it remains open all day. A beautiful white handbag! You didn't realise? When you know me better, you'll appreciate that shoes and handbags are my weakness.

We've enjoyed our stroll up La Rambla. We each had an iced coffee and then did some shopping. As I've said before, the ports we visit mean different things to different people, and as you tick various destinations off your list in Barcelona, it'll mean different things to you too.

But we must get on now. Goodbye Barcel-**Oh**-na until the next time! We have an invitation to drinks with the Captain this evening and we don't want to be late.

Tonight's Dress Code is Informal. To quote P&O in *Aurora Today*, 'lounge suit, jacket and tie or smart shirt with linen or blazer style jacket for gentlemen. Cocktail or day dress for the ladies'.

It's not often that the men's dress code is longer than the ladies'! Even in the time we have been serious cruisers, dress codes have become much less formal. A few years ago every lady wore a full-length dress on a Formal Night. Nowadays evening trouser suits have become popular and the number of Formal Evenings on each cruise has been reduced. Even the dress codes in the Queen's Grill on the *Queen Elizabeth 2*, where every night used to be a Formal Night, have been relaxed, but casual nights in the Grill Rooms have not yet made an appearance.

As mentioned at the beginning of this cruise, Himself is spoiling me and we have a suite. One of the perks with a suite is often an invitation from the Captain to join him for cocktails or, as happened on one occasion, afternoon tea in Andersons, the comfortable, *frightfully* English bar, complete with marble fireplace and arm chairs – a sort of stately home sitting room afloat. These invitations are special as the small numbers invited mean opportunities for proper conversation with the Captain and his senior officers, instead of a quick 'Hello' and a smile for the inevitable camera.

This reception is being held in the Pennant Bar at the rear of the Orangery – a wonderful setting overlooking the stern of *Aurora* – so tonight I'll wear my trouser suit. Even though it's been a lovely temperature all day, once the ship is moving again, it can become quite cool on the open decks and more than one goose pimple will be in evidence by the time we're summoned for our *splendid* or *tremendous* evening on board.

This evening in the Curzon Theatre there's comedian Roy Walker, in Carmens the illusionist Richard Griffin, and in the Playhouse two classical music performances, followed by a romantic comedy film at 22.45 – assuming you can stay awake that long. Tomorrow is a long awaited and very welcome day at sea.

No port, no excursion, no pressure to do anything but breathe – and of course enjoy the odd mouthful of food.

13

NEPTUNE AT SEA

Thank goodness for that! It's a sea day... 24 hours of utter peace and quiet with absolutely no pressure to do anything, and it's just what we all need after the last five days. Are you feeling exhausted too? All that rushing about, trying to cram as much into each port visit as possible – are you beginning to feel like the Japanese doing Europe... today is Wednesday so it must be France? Yesterday was Italy and tomorrow will be Spain. I doubt that Mr and Mrs F.T.C. will surface until lunchtime!

Sunrise was at 06.45 but few, if any, on board will have noticed except for the dependable chaps on the Bridge who have been watching over the ship whilst we passengers slept.

Although we will enjoy ours in the cabin as usual, Breakfast in the Orangery goes on until 11.00. Few passengers will arrive for the 07.00 start, and by late morning those determined souls who are beginning to think about lunch will find themselves trampled under foot by cereal-bearing, weary but hungry passengers, desperately trying to clear the sleep from their eyes. Go on! You're on holiday! Turn over and go back to sleep… I shall whisper the next bit so as not to disturb you.

* * * * *

Today is a very special day; in fact it's probably unique. We on board *Aurora* are at sea somewhere between Barcelona and Praia da Rocha in Portugal and the very last place any of you want to think about is Southampton. However, back there this evening the Princess Royal and her daughter Zara Phillips are going to name the latest additions to the P&O fleet, *Adonia* and *Oceana*. It's not every day that a ship is named, and certainly for two to be named at the same time to join the same fleet has to be unique. A lot of publicity material has dropped through our letter box at home about *The White Sisters*, as they are known, and we've been watching it all with interest as we're booked to go on *Adonia* in May to Iceland, and *Oceana* in September to Venice… I did tell you that cruising was addictive, didn't I? And if you add to all that a three week trip on the *Queen Elizabeth 2* to the Caribbean in November, you'll begin to see why I'm forever on a diet when my feet do touch the ground in Southampton.

This evening in Carmen's and Champions we can watch these ships being named, always assuming that the magic that is satellite communication doesn't let us down. If you've other plans for this evening, you'll be able to see the celebrations all day tomorrow on your in-cabin television. Not only that, but we on board *Aurora* can guess the weight of the cake, now on display in the Atrium on deck five, and possibly win a bottle of bubbly. No, you can't pick the cake up as it's just too big, and no, we don't know if it's a fruit cake or sponge, but there's nothing to stop you doing multiple entries! And if you don't win the bottle of bubbly, you can always enjoy two '*White Sisters*' Cocktails for the price of one, although you'll have to ask at the bar to find out what they contain.

* * * * *

On a sea day, life on board cruise ships carries on regardless of how many passengers attend the advertised events. I wasn't up to see how many walked a mile at 08.00 and neither did I attend the Yoga with Shaun at 09.00. I suspect the usual Line Dancing fanatics joined Sarah at 10.00 for her thigh slapping and foot stomping class. Luckily on *Aurora* the Deck Quoits and Shuffle-board are held at the aft end of deck 13, so no avoidance tactics are necessary for those walking gently around Promenade deck, which was all Himself and I felt up to this morning. At 11.15 in the Crystal Dome there is an ice carving demonstration and if you've never seen it done before, it is well worth going along to watch. Starting with a *gynormous* block of ice, and in front of the assembled passengers, this brave chap from the catering department attacks the block with various implements to the 'oooohs' and 'aaaaahs' of those who've never held anything larger than an ice cube out of their ice box at home. Chips of ice fly this way and that, as the object begins to take shape.

"What's it going to be?"

"A bird?"

"A fish?"

You'll have to read on to find out.

Bing Bong! "Good afternoon Ladies and Gentlemen.

This is the Officer of the Watch speaking from the Bridge. The time is 12 noon."

(Here follows several rings on the ship's bell so any passengers not totally brain dead by now, can check the setting on their watches, just in case they should miss the start of lunch by thirty seconds!)

"Since leaving Barcelona yesterday evening," the Officer continues, "Aurora has steamed a total distance of 344 nautical miles at an average speed of 19.1 knots. Throughout the morning *Aurora* continued on various south-westerly courses to parallel the Spanish Coast and we will shortly set a westerly course towards the Gibraltar Straits. At 20.00 this evening, we will pass the Rock of Gibraltar and three hours later we will clear the Straits and set a north westerly course towards Praia da Rocha."

He then goes on to give our position, longitude and latitude, the wind direction and force and the temperature on the open decks. It is very reassuring that someone knows just where we are, as we passengers are quite beyond caring, lulled as we have been into a relaxed holiday stupor!

* * * * *

Did you ever have to write lines at school? Anyone who did will know what a pointless pastime they were. They taught me nothing, except possibly how to hold three pens in one hand and therefore scribble three almost illegible lines at the same time, and all they actually did was waste my time or stop me doing my homework.

Today I will be good and not overeat. Today I will be good and not overeat. Today I will be...

You'll see what I mean!

A sensible breakfast this morning and no morning

coffee. Water, just water. That's all I need.

"There's Neptune's seafood buffet lunch by the pool today," Himself breaks into my thoughts.

Advertised in the daily programme in *Aurora Today*, these delicacies are hard to miss.

"Shall we have just a small lunch?" he asks.

"Why not!" I shrug my shoulders.

Why not? Because anything small when it comes to food is almost impossible to find on board *Aurora*.

Neptune's buffet is large – what an understatement. The centrepiece is a vast cooked salmon with a surprised look on its face, its skin peeled away and replaced by cucumber and aspic, its mouth open as if it's just said 'ouch'! I doubt it enjoyed the experience.

Behind him, newly born in the ice carving demonstration earlier today, (which hopefully you were watching) is a vast, icy salmon appearing to leap seawards, and now glistening in the sun as it slowly melts. It's actually spinning slowly on its turntable, and is destined to be stored in the ice carving freezer after the remains of the buffet have been cleared away. P&O employ a specialist ice carver to create the most wonderful displays and load huge blocks of ice for that purpose before they leave Southampton, as we found on our recent tour of the stores.

As with most buffets, you start at one end, having queued of course, and work your way slowly past all the delicious delicacies on offer. Hunger has set in during your time in the queue and all the resolve of this morning has vanished with every minute that has passed. Fellow passengers wander past in search of seats, some with huge dinner plates piled precariously high with seafood.

There are, of course, plenty of passengers with quite

normal appetites, but they'd make boring reading. Who among you would really want to hear about the slim blonde with an hourglass figure who was wearing a tiny red bikini, a pretty wrap covering her legs, much to the sadness of Himself and the other men in the queue? A multitude of attractive swimming costumes is in evidence, every colour from black to white – and that's not only the men – as passengers take the opportunity to top up their tans before we start our journey north up the side of Portugal. Everyone is enjoying this relaxing sea day on board *Aurora*.

"Sea food's not fattening, is it?" the man in front of me asks his wife.

I wonder why he's chosen odd socks to wear with his sandals – possibly as he can't see his feet, he doesn't realise how colourful he is.

"The prawns in mayonnaise are a bit naughty love, but you're on holiday. Enjoy yourself. Might as well get your money's worth."

They laugh to each other and start to place the food carefully on their empty plates.

I watch as he takes just a little salmon and cod bake, hot of course, a few fish goujons, only one salmon and broccoli fish cake, followed by a small spoonful of kedgeree.

"My plate's full love," says Mr Odd Socks. "Where can I put the cold buffet?"

"Put it on top of course," Mrs Odd Socks laughs. "It all goes down the same way," helping herself to half a bagel piled high with smoked salmon.

She reached for some more smoked salmon as if designing a skyscraper, and just a small spoonful of caviar on top – the red stuff, not the black. Can you imagine 1,800 passengers helping themselves to vast quantities of black caviar? The company's profits would sink.

"Don't forget the prawns love," she adds. "Try not to get too much mayonnaise."

"Did you get a crab?" Mr Odd Socks is determined his beloved will not miss out. He helps her to a filled crab shell that sits precariously on top of the smoked salmon bagel, topped with caviar, now acting as glue on the bottom of the shell.

"Can I have another please?" he asks the chef serving the king prawns. "On here," he points to the top of his filled crab as the chef tries desperately to find a landing ground for his double offering of enormous prawns.

Slowly they walk to an empty table, and I follow swiftly to take up residence at their table as it's in the shade, my plate looking positively *anorexic* by comparison.

"On a diet are we?" Mr Odd Socks laughs at me as he extracts the first king prawn from its rigid jacket and dunks the end into a large blob of thick mayonnaise I'd not seen him add to his plate.

The heat from the salmon and cod bake is making the dollop begin to run over the side of the plate and onto the table.

"She's a great cook," he wipes the mayonnaise off his chin and nods to his wife: "but she don't serve up food like this at home."

"It's back to the diet next week," Mrs Odd Socks smiles at us.

"Better enjoy it whilst I can, eh?" he grins as he attacks his filled crab.

The shell of the now absent crab is deposited on the table, held in place by the pool of melted mayonnaise. I find it difficult to look at him as I wonder if my smoked salmon looks the same as his does, chewed as it is throughout his conversation.

"Where did you get that salad?" he asks as I cut into a beautifully ripe tomato.

"You don't want none of that stuff," Mrs Odd Socks interrupts us. "They're always saying not to eat salad abroad," she continues. "You never know where it's been or who's touched it. You can catch worms from it, or even typhoid."

"I don't think they mean here on board ship," I try not to laugh as I concentrate intently on my crisp lettuce and cucumber.

His prawns are disappearing accompanied by the now tepid fish pie and kedgeree.

"Delicious! Really great," Mr Odd Socks says, helping the few remaining mayonnaise drowned prawns onto his fork with a large piece of bread. Licking his fingers, he adds: "What's for pudding love?"

Believe it or not, that's OK with me. He took a huge quantity but he ate and enjoyed every mouthful, and then did an Oliver! Pudding duly arrived – that should read in the plural – courtesy of Mrs Odd Socks, and was duly disposed of by them both with the same delight.

The people who upset me are the *plate-pilers* who take great quantities of everything and leave half of it behind at the end of the meal. Heaven knows what some of the chefs must think when they see the piles of discarded food. All the waste food is eventually ground down and disposed of at sea, far away from land, although the surprised poached salmon, which escaped the attention of Mr Odd Socks and his wife, is now probably destined to end its life as fish cakes for tomorrow. Something about the poor sea creatures in the sea below us eating tiny pieces of their distant relatives, complete with Tartar

Sauce makes me remember a supposed cause of Mad Cow's Disease!

Lunch, as with all the food on board *Aurora*, was delicious. Had we chosen to avoid the Neptune's buffet, there was plenty of other choice available to us. The main restaurant, where we would have had a three-course lunch with waiter service, Café Bordeaux which serves food 24 hours a day but has a limited menu, the normal hot and cold buffet luncheon in the Orangery, or indeed room service. On an A-Z of cruising, S for Starvation would never appear.

Today I will be good and not overeat. Today I WILL be good and not overeat. Today I…

I'm doing really well.

Lunch was modest – a smoked salmon bagel, small mayonnaise prawns, a little caviar and some salad followed by a fruit jelly – no cream of course! – at 14.00.

So why at 17.00 when our canapés arrive in the suite do I feel hungry? Three canapés, two chocolates, and a couple of chocolate biscuits later, washed down with a cup of tea, I announce to Himself: "I'll give afternoon tea a miss today!"

"Will you last out until dinner at 20.30?" he asks with a smile.

* * * * *

Port out, starboard home – the sun is now on our side of the ship. Here in the Mediterranean it's nearly 19.00. The sea resembles blueberry soup as we slip slowly on towards the Straits of Gibraltar and the Atlantic Ocean. Dolphins frolic, seaweed slithers, on board everywhere passengers shower and dress for dinner. At this point there is a choice… to dress or to stay where we are, cosseted on our balcony, away from all temptation.

But that would be too easy and unkind to our fellow table mates with whom we have cheerful conversation each evening. No doubt a telephone call would follow.

"Are you OK? Are you ill? Why did you miss dinner?"

So tonight we'll succumb – but only two courses… well, OK three, but no chocolate after dinner.

Today I will be good and not overeat. Today I will… or maybe tomorrow!

* * * * *

So what shall we do this evening? How about going to the pictures – Oscar nominated *About Schmidt* with Jack Nicholson is showing in the Playhouse – I must tell Terry, our Jack Nicholson look-alike. From London musicals *Sunset Boulevard* and *Copacabana*, Petrina Johnson is singing in Carmen's and in the Curzon Theatre Richard Baker is introducing a Classical Operetta Evening. We don't feel bright enough tonight for the Syndicate Quiz, or energetic enough for Strict Tempo Dancing in Masquerades. These sea days are quite exhausting! What about a quiet drink in the Crow's Nest on Deck 13, watching the lights of Southern Spain in the distance as we join the traffic in this busy waterway and navigate our way through the Straits and into the cooler water of the Atlantic? You never know, the Captain on the Bridge may need our help!

* * * * *

Sitting in the comfortable armchairs in the Crow's Nest, a Lumbar Rumba in my hand – the Cocktail of the Day made of Midori, Malibu, Crème de Banana, Pineapple juice, and Sweet and Sour Mix – Himself is studying *Aurora Today*.

"Wait a minute! I've just noticed. We get an extra hour tonight! Ship's clocks will be put BACK one hour to GMT + 1 at 02.00 tomorrow morning!" Himself announces cheerfully, reading from today's information.

"Whoopee!" I give him a hug.

"Suddenly I've got some energy. Let's go and have another drink!"

And have an *unbelievable* or *versatile* evening on board.

14

OUR LAST PORT OF CALL

– or the ups and downs of Portugal.

Well! What can I say? It's out there, our last port of call before Southampton on Sunday. After that, all that's left is… but no! We'll come to that later – in the next chapter.

Praia da Rocha is an old friend. Himself and I first came here in 1980 something, fairly newly married and in search of some peace and quiet, sun, sea and sex, but not necessarily in that order. I have the photographs in front of me as I write. I see a bronzed body, darker hair and a great pair of legs – and that's only Himself. Did he really wear shorts that, well, short? Wow! How memories grow dim. And there's me – much lighter in weight, skin still the palest of pinks, Factor 30 shouting out from every inch of uncovered flesh, posing like a film star, bottom on a rock – no doubt having been checked for creepy crawlies first – feet dabbling in the warm water lapping at the base of my throne. The sunglasses mask my romantic gaze as I look into the camera held by my adoring husband. Ah yes, I remember it well. Those were the days in Praia da Rocha.

We'd decided on a week away on the spur of the moment and Himself had telephoned the hotel. You did that in those days as booking on the internet was unheard of – we didn't even have a computer. Telephones were quite complicated enough for us.

"A sea view room with *large* double bed," Himself had shouted at the girl on the end of the telephone – well Portugal was a long way away and he's never really come to terms with these new fangled instruments.

"We'll be arriving on the 16th May."

A pause whilst the girl checked the availability.

"No – just bed and breakfast please," Himself shouted his reply to her question.

Another pause, whilst I sat in his study trying to hear the other side of the conversation.

"Wonderful. Just to confirm, we have a room for two with *large* double bed, with breakfast and sea view. Arriving on the 16th."

So I jumped up and down with delight – I *was* younger in those days – whilst Himself provided credit card details – oh yes! – we did have those way back in the 1980s!

And his final, loud, comment to her?

"Our flight doesn't get in until late, so we won't be at the hotel until nearly **midnight**," emphasising the word *midnight.*

"You won't let our room to anyone else, will you?"

But of course they did.

Tired from the pre-holiday organisation and the flight, we arrived more than ready for our *large* double bed and in no mood to be told 'there is no room at the inn'. Our room had indeed been let to another couple, only an hour earlier.

"We thought you were not coming," said the male receptionist with the slow, correct pronunciation of a person not speaking his native language. "And it was very late that we gave the room to someone else."

To cut a long story short, and following our threat to sleep in the foyer of the Hotel Algarve, having first changed into jimjams and new sexy nightie, the Manager was called. He spoke fluent English. Which is how we found ourselves waking up in the best suite in the Hotel the following morning.

"Only for four nights," the Manager had grinned at us, as he swept his dark wavy hair back off his bronzed forehead with a hand heavy with gold rings.

"There will be a sea view room in the main hotel after that, and we have it reserved, just for you."

And with a wave of his gold rings, he disappeared behind the scenes, never to be seen again by us.

Breakfast arrived as ordered. We yawned and stretched and turned over in our *large* double bed and promptly returned to sleep.

Some hours later, and following the persistent knocking of the chambermaid, the cold coffee and now leathery croissants were eaten on the balcony overlooking the sea. And this is the point at which we first began to realise just where we were.

Overlooking the sea, indeed we were, but from what a height. We were sitting on the edge of a cliff, which rose vertically some 30 feet high above the wide, deserted sandy beach below.

Our enormous suite comprised the large bedroom complete with *huge* double bed, an equally spacious sitting room, vast bathroom and long, cool hallway...the whole suite finished off by this balcony...although it was much more than a boring old balcony. Enormous, large, huge, vast – I've run out of superlatives – everything seemed so large in those days! – so just let's say the balcony was big. Although the word *balcony* doesn't correctly describe it either, as the base of this balcony was actually on the cliff top, so I guess the word terrace comes to mind. A foot more of cliff top beyond the edge of our terrace, and the world disappeared, leaving open space and just the view of row upon row of empty beach chairs in the distance and the gently lapping sea beyond. The cliff top grasses and plants peeping over the edge of the terrace gave the impression of being in a pasture and because of the wall at either end, it was totally private, at least we hoped it was. Passers by on the beach below would have needed binoculars to intrude upon our privacy!

Praia da Rocha in those days was bliss – little more than a small seaside resort with a massive beach, and a small beach restaurant that looked shabby during the day but took on an air of romance after dark, the lanterns hanging from the wooden poles casting shadows and softening the sunburnt faces of the assembled diners. How we enjoyed those romantic dinners... the seafood... the wine... the soft music... the cool of the evening following the heat of the day... the stars glimmering above... the lack of knowledge of the hygiene standards inside of the restaurant kitchen, glimpses of which could be seen through a shabby wooden door, the only entrance to the kitchen. We contented ourselves with the fact that the wine would kill the bugs, and after all, everything was piping hot – except for the salad!

Our days were spent strolling along the golden sand,

still virtually empty of tourists, and sheltering from the sun in the caves at the end which formed a walkway through to the next beach. Swimming in the hotel's warm pool before enjoying a leisurely lunch during which Himself tried to teach the hotel's parrot a few choice words of English became the norm. Wine at lunchtime had the inevitable result, and each day we'd retire for our siesta to our *large* double bed.

On our last day in the suite, the combination of the heavy lunch, the wine and the sun, which always makes me feel sexy, added to the comments from Himself about the seclusion of the terrace, we substituted the deluxe comfort of the Algarve's bed for the wooden boards in the sun. Re-reading that, we were obviously much younger and more than a little inebriated!

From my vantage point as I turned my head, I could see the towering cactus flowers high above me, and the waves of the Atlantic breaking on the beach far below. In the water rushed, and out it flowed back into the sea meeting up with the next wave. In and out, in and out... the creaking boards the only accompaniment to our afternoon siesta, as the seagulls flew overhead and cawed as they glanced down at these mad English tourists.

"Only mad dogs and Englishmen go out in the noonday sun!" I sang softly, nuzzling into Himself's hair.

"It's 15.00." he glanced at his watch... but he had removed his socks.

We froze.

"What was that?" I whispered.

"Someone on the balcony next door!" he hissed.

"That was a moan," I added.

"What **do** you think *they* are doing?" Himself grinned. "Disgusting! They just don't know who might be listening!"

Carefully, avoiding the squeaking board, we extricated ourselves and retired to the shade of the bedroom for the last time before taking up residence in the standard double with sea view.

Life would never be quite the same at the Hotel Algarve again, with or without a balcony!

* * * * *

Today, standing on *Aurora's* balcony, I gaze across the calm water to the ribbon of concrete that is modern Praia da Rocha. It bears little resemblance to the place of our romantic interlude in the eighties... a great reminder that it is often a mistake to go back!

We've chosen to go on a trip to the End of Europe today and really ought to be in the Curzon Theatre, getting our stickers and joining our group. Praia da Rocha is a tender port and the noise of our lifeboats being lowered after we had dropped our anchor approximately a mile off shore, ensured that no passengers would sleep through breakfast this morning.

For we passengers on tours, it's relatively simple – queue in the Curzon Theatre no later than 08.25 and get a sticker. Queue to get on the tender when our group is called. Once on shore, we then queue to get onto our allocated bus for the trip, and off we go.

For passengers wishing to go ashore independently, and there will be many, they should meet in Carmen's from 09.00 onwards. All the tour passengers will disembark first and it will not be until towards 10.00 that independent passengers will be able to board a tender for the 15 minute trip to the landing stage near Portimao. From here they will be able to catch a shuttle service which will take them into Praia da Rocha, tickets for which should have been purchased from Reception on board by last night.

Thankfully our journey to Sagres uses the new road and saves us having to spoil our memories further by driving through the concrete blocks that have now become an anonymous Portuguese resort. More than one passenger nods off, trying to recoup the sleep lost by too much partying last night.

Cabo de Sao Vicente is named after St. Vincent whose body was allegedly washed ashore here and his presumed remains now rest in Lisbon's Cathedral. Cape St. Vincent with its 200 feet high granite cliffs facing the Atlantic, is the most southwest point of Portugal – between it and America there is nothing but sea. The coastline of this part of the Algarve is spectacular with high jagged cliffs, great chunks of which have been eroded by the elements over millions of years and by the pounding Atlantic breakers. The danger for shipping is obvious and right on the end of Cape St. Vincent stands a lighthouse which was to be our destination today.

Like a coach load of Japanese tourists, we jump off the bus, rush to the edge, peer over at the crashing waves below pounding the base of the cliff, say 'cheese' as our photographs are taken and rush back onto the coach for the next short ride to our coffee stop. A few of us stop and buy local honey, almonds and dried figs, but most are now intent upon a late breakfast of coffee and almond cookies. I doubt they'd have been called cookies years ago before tourism invaded Europe, but they do taste exceptionally good – breakfast for the intrepid *Aurora* explorer was a hurried affair this morning!

On our journey back to the ship we have our third stop and visit Lagos with its sturdy medieval walls and narrow bustling streets and spend time in the Chapel of

Santo Antonio with its intricate carvings covered in gold leaf. There is no time to walk around the city walls on this trip, and a quick peep at the old Slave Market followed by an ice cream has to suffice. Lagos, unlike Praia da Rocha, has maintained its beauty despite a few occasional dollops from the concrete mixer.

But the fun is yet to begin. Had *Aurora* been tied up next to the quayside as in many ports we visit, we would have jumped off the coach and walked up the gangway, back into the cool of the air conditioned interior. Not today. I know it was early this morning, but do you remember getting the tender from the ship's side for the 15 minute trip to the landing point? We now have to make that return journey. It's noon. It's hot. Many of the tour buses appear to have returned at the same time. There is a long queue.

Himself mutters. He is prone to muttering at times like this.

"Bad organisation... too hot to stand... elderly people... no seating... " but mentally I've switched him off as *I* am prone to do at times like this and look instead at the brightly coloured fishing boats tied up near our queue.

Bundles of nets rolled up and left in heaps, red fenders hanging over the side to prevent damage, the sun beating down on the blue and white boats as they bob up and down in the water.

The queue moves forward, slowly like an exhausted snake half-baked in the noonday oven.

"We'll be on the next one," I try to pacify Himself who looks decidedly weary.

Some staff members from *Aurora* have started to distribute water... how would we all have coped in a desert situation? Obviously news of our long queue has reached important ears, and several more lifeboats can be seen making their way steadily towards us. Suddenly we're afloat, sandwiched together in the lifeboat like sardines and are being gazed down upon by those less fortunate than ourselves, who still stand in the queue on shore.

"Where shall we have lunch?" Himself has recovered his appetite!

"Café Bordeaux," I reply where guess what, they have sardines on the menu!

* * * * *

And now, back on board, whilst Himself recuperates from his exhausting coach trip, and others are still dashing about on shore in the heat of the afternoon sun, I'm off for some real indulgence!

Reflexology is not available on every cruise, but when it is, I try to have at least one session. These treatments are very popular and need to be booked well in advance.

"Just relax," she says as my right foot is first to receive the attention.

"Mmmmm," I reply – or at least I think I do, as I'm already slipping into doze mode.

"Mmmm."

"Mmmm."

"Mmmm."

Some time later when I reluctantly wake up, I sign the bill which will be debited to my ship's account, I tip the Reflexologist and quietly depart. I can't explain what it is about reflexology that leaves me feeling so utterly relaxed and at peace with the world, but it does. Returning to our balcony, now in the shade, I continue my doze as our tenders rush to and fro, returning weary passengers to this haven of peace.

* * * * *

Come on. Wake up! We've lots to do.

Tonight in the Theatre *Aurora's* own Theatre Company present Elvis, The Musical.

In Carmen's there's music throughout the 60s, 70s, 80s and 90s – I presume that's decades and not ages of passengers on board! And in the Playhouse Meryl Streep stars in *The Hours* at 20.00 and at 22.00 *The Lord of The Rings, The Two Towers* is being shown. Let's go and have today's Cocktail of the Day and watch us sail away from our last port of call. A mixture of vodka, peach schnapps, Grenadine and orange juice, called 'Fun on the Beach', should set the evening off on the right note as we round the point of Cape St. Vincent and head up the west coast of Portugal.

"Aaaaaaa Lisbon," I sigh.

"I know what you're thinking about," Himself laughs.

"Handbags and shoes?"

"Well thank goodness we're giving it a miss this cruise," he adds as he passes me a canapé to enjoy with my drink.

"Thank goodness we're giving Cascais a miss too," I bounce back at him.

"Touché!" is all he can add to that comment.

* * * * *

Cascais, and another trip in the eighties... we were 'in to' Portugal in those days, or at least we were until that fateful trip. We've visited Cascais since, when we've docked at Lisbon on previous cruises, catching the train that runs along the length of the coastline, but it's not the same either. Gone is the tiny fishing village we enjoyed. They still fish from there of course, but tourism has changed the quaintness of the village and turned it into a town like many others.

We'd spent a whole week overindulging on seafood. Seafood this, and seafood that. We'd eaten it in so many forms that we were ready for a change.

"Remember that girl you sat next to on the plane?" Himself had asked. "She told us about a restaurant not far from here which we should visit. Let's go this evening."

So we did. A taxi drive to a long, deserted beach in the middle of which, high on stilts and totally made of dark wood, was a romantic restaurant. The sun was setting on the horizon – well it always does, doesn't it? Just as the hero and heroine arrive, hand in hand, the blood red sun begins to sink beneath the horizon. So we arranged for the taxi to return for us some hours later, and stood and watched the sun set.

Whenever we visit some foreign restaurant and the menu is not in English, Himself always seems to have the knack of selecting the most delicious item on that menu. I always end up with something pale and insipid and have to pretend it's absolutely wonderful.

But not today. I was determined. In my bag was a dictionary and as soon as the menu arrived I immersed myself in the task of extracting something utterly exquisite to prove that two could play at that game!

"I'll have a... ", and here my Portuguese totally escapes me!

"What's that?" Himself was amazed not to have been asked my usual question of 'what can I have?'

"Roast suckling pig," I shrugged my shoulders,

fluttered my eyelashes, replaced the dictionary in my bag and prepared myself for delicious pork complete with crackling and hopefully beautifully cooked vegetables.

"Wow! Now I really *am* impressed! But I'm having some fish," he grinned.

The restaurant was dark. The wooden walls were dark. The lights were very dim. Romantic? Maybe… but difficult when it came to eating. However, difficult it may have been, but there was absolutely no disguising what I had on my plate. Roast suckling pig the dictionary may have said. Cold pork chop was what I actually got. The fish looked delicious. We passed on puds, enjoyed a quick coffee and caught our taxi back to Cascais.

That was Wednesday evening.

Saturday morning we were leaving for the airport and just grabbing a quick breakfast when it happened. I felt sick.

I shall omit the next few hours, but suffice it to say I was not very well. Not very well throughout the dreadful journey to the airport. Not very well in the airport building. Not very well throughout the flight home where the Steward obviously recognised the problem and moved all the passengers forward leaving Himself and the patient alone in the rear cabin of the aircraft. And definitely not very well when we were collected at Heathrow by Himself's daughter.

"I've got food poisoning," I gritted my teeth before rushing off to the loo again.

"Don't be so dramatic," Himself's comments barely reached me in my dash for sanctuary.

"She's just got an upset stomach!" although as he'd turned grey in the middle of the flight, he too felt a little, how shall I put it, unstable!

Our GP visited and following tests, into which we need not go, visited every day thereafter for several weeks, jabbing my posterior with his needle in an attempt to stop me vomiting.

We both had salmonella.

My parents were very helpful and sent cuttings from their newspaper about a tourist who had recently returned from Portugal with salmonella and had died. That made us both feel a lot better. Himself recovered more quickly, having had a lighter dose of the food poisoning, presumably caught from me when he'd kissed me goodnight… oh come on! We were on holiday after all!

The Public Health Inspector visited. Apparently the doctor has to notify his office of cases of salmonella, not that this piece of information made me feel any better. I was now a shadow of my former self, and getting thinner.

"What did you eat on Friday night?" Himself was asked.

"And on Thursday?"

"And on Wednesday?"

"Aaaaah!" said the Public Health Inspector when he learnt of the cold pork chop. "It's unlikely to have been the seafood – much more likely to be cold meats or cream," the man told us for future reference.

Do vegetarians get salmonella? I wonder. Remind me to leave my dictionary behind in future. Three months later I was pronounced clear of the bug, having consumed vast quantities of raw garlic which apparently is a natural disinfectant. I don't know how true that is, but certainly no-one wanted to get near me during this recovery time when even my perfume couldn't mask the smell!

* * * * *

And that brings me neatly to another problem. Norwalk Virus. Now anyone who reads a newspaper has heard of it. The media are delighted to report the problem, also known as the '24 hour stomach bug'.

You can get it anywhere in the world of course, but it's far more dramatic when passengers on a ship are infected. As we were told in a hand-out by P&O :

> **Norwalk Virus** *is so widespread that only the common cold is reported more frequently. It is highly contagious and thus easily passed from person to person.*

They went on to remind us of preventative measures such as washing hands frequently and to avoid touching our mouths.

In the unlikely event of being affected by the virus, now officially classified as Norovirus, you merely get in touch with the Medical Centre on board, who will come to your rescue at no charge! (Sail with P&O where you can be sick for free... but only with the Norwalk Virus!). Plenty of antiseptic hand wipes have been in evidence during the cruise, and, as always, the whole ship has been kept in a spotless condition. So just keep washing those hands – it's amazing how many people don't!

Exhaustion is setting in. Let's give the entertainment a miss tonight. All this talk of *large* beds has made me tired.

Do have a *wonderfully eXstatic* evening on board... so who cares if I cheat a little?

15

CALLING ALL CHOCOHOLICS

The news has obviously spread far beyond the ship, but they'd better hurry or they'll be late and miss it. It starts at 15.45 and only goes on for one hour. Was that why the whale was spotted this lunchtime swimming alongside *Aurora*? Obviously she was trying to get to the front of the queue that is already beginning to form. Look! See! There are some more – three of them, all heading in the same direction. Does a Dolphin have a sweet tooth? Now what? A flock of seabirds flying alongside – will there be any to spare for them? Possibly a crumb or two! It depends how many attend, but normally it's packed out.

There's great excitement on Deck 6 as we join the babble of chattering passengers that has formed into a very orderly crocodile. Orderly, that is, until two unfortunate ladies come up the stairs from Deck 5 below, and quietly try to sneak in towards the front of the queue.

On the whole, we British are content to queue, but

this holds true only so long as no-one tries to edge in and commit the sin of queue jumping. A mutiny threatens. A few angry comments are made. A waiter quickly steps forward and very politely addresses the two now red faced, embarrassed ladies.

"The queue starts up there, ladies," and he indicates the queue, the end of which cannot be seen from where we stand.

Every face is now looking at them, as they look back at the queue that disappears up the next flight of stairs and beyond, each stair four deep with eager passengers, each flight of stairs has at least ten steps. I estimate that well over a third of all passengers here on board *Aurora* are intent on not missing IT.

Most of us have seen IT all before – probably several times! Been there, done that, possibly even got the t-shirt, and definitely got the extra inches, but there's something addictive about this part of cruising. This is one occasion not to be missed.

But first we enter the unseen and, I'm sad to say, the often un-thought-about world of the Galley – kitchen, to all of you still not converted to nautical terms. But before that we have to face another official photograph. I pause for a moment with Jean and Mrs F.T.C. beside two beautiful swans, one swan delicately carved out of golden butter and the other a magnificent ice carving.

"Smile please," the photographer asks us unnecessarily, for we are now all conditioned to smile at the first sight of any camera, having spent nearly a fortnight of 'Smile please!'

We clutch the piece of paper we have just been handed entitled 'Galley Visit and Chocoholic's Buffet'. There! I've said the word! Chocolate! Can you smell it yet? Do you know anybody who doesn't like chocolate of at least one variety, dark, milk or white?

But let us concentrate for a while longer. The Galley. As our leaflet tells us, *Aurora's* main galley is rather larger than our kitchens at home. But then it would need to be, wouldn't it? When did you last cater for up to 1,900 guests – even in two sittings? Most of the 116,500 main meals consumed in a typical two-week cruise are cooked in this galley, which serves both of *Aurora's* restaurants. Every plate of food for the Medina Restaurant leaves from one side and for the Alexandria Restaurant from the other side, with all the cooking area in the middle.

Looking at the map on the flat piece of paper in my hand, words like Plate House Aft and Plate House Forward are separated by Pot Wash – they take up the port side of the galley – obviously the lines on the chart just don't convey the size of this area.

We enter through the Medina Restaurant, eyes rapidly adjusting following the latest flash from the photographer's equipment. Most people want to keep going, knowing what awaits them in the Alexandria Restaurant, and I feel irritation as I try to linger and gaze over the stainless steel work surfaces. As I said before, there is a tremendous amount of stainless steel on this ship.

A cold area for cheeses, starters, cold meats and salads – a massive bakery area with a gynormous food mixer that makes my little Kenwood look as though it belongs in a doll's house. This is where all the delicious bread and rolls are made each day, and is next to a vast Pastry Section where 21 people work, preparing all the fattening desserts we've been eating without a second thought about the effort involved in getting that blob of cream to sit just *so*! This is where the majority of the damage to our figures has been caused. I have certainly consumed more than my fair share of the 42,000 afternoon cakes and pastries 70,000 rolls and 3,600 loaves of bread baked on this cruise!

The amount of food consumed on board is stupendous. 15 tons of meat, four tons of fish, seven tons of poultry and game, three and a half tons of bacon, ham and gammon, 28 tons of fresh fruit and vegetables. Figures that are indeed mind-boggling! 51,000 eggs – picture a box of six and keep multiplying – 10,500 litres of milk and 4,000 litres of ice cream. Just imagine the size of their supermarket checkout receipt! Just imagine the size of their supermarket trolley!

The galley is, of course, at the moment almost empty and absolutely spotless, a sea of stainless steel. I close my eyes and try to imagine it in the middle of second sitting for dinner tonight – the Captain's Gala Dinner. A waiter picking up my starter of wild boar terrine with Armagnac and prunes en croute, or will I choose the deep fried Camembert served with walnut and apple salsa? I should, of course, go for the prawn and melon, the slimming choice, but I won't. The diet can wait until next week – but I will pass on the soup tonight.

It's impossible to visualise the endless plates of King Fish, Saddle of Lamb, Pan fried Calves Liver and Roast Pheasant so I concentrate on what will be my choice – a plate of Courgette and Aubergine Fritter on a Lentil and Potato Cake with an Avocado and Tomato Salsa. The vegetarian food has been superb in variety, quality and presentation, but regrettably not slimming.

Or shall I forgo it all and have one of everything from the dessert menu?

Apple Tarte Tatin with vanilla Ice Cream.

Mango Flavoured Crème Brulee.

Vanilla, Coffee and Tropical Fruit Ice Creams.

Sweet Sauces of Butterscotch, Chocolate and Melba.
Fresh Fruit Salad – how boring.

Or a selection of chocolate desserts, although after the next hour will anybody choose that option?

A few of the chefs are on hand to answer questions and I catch sight of one guy preparing the canapés that will arrive in the cabins later this afternoon.

This galley only caters for the passengers, and on the deck below is the galley used to prepare the meals for the 850 crew. On the two decks below that of course are the enormous larders, fridges and freezers that I told you about, where all the provisions are stored for the voyage.

The eager crocodile edges steadily forward, tongues licking lips in anticipation, past the soup, meat, fish, sauce and vegetable sections, past the pastry sections and out through the other entrance towards the Alexandria restaurant. I can smell it now. A wave of excitement ripples through the queue. The lady behind gives me a little shove – I'm delaying the queue – there might not be any left.

Our restaurant, normally empty at this time of day and laid elegantly for first sitting for this evening's dinner, is almost full. Our crocodile entering through the lower entrance designed for wheel chair passengers and those who wish to avoid any steps, takes precedence, and having toured the Galley, we're each handed a large, white dinner plate.

"You can take it back to your cabin Madam," the Restaurant Manager says with a tolerant smile.

She's seen it all before – once on every cruise – and must wonder why we're not all sick after what we've consumed already during this cruise.

We edge forward slowly, cameras flashing, hands using tongs to select an item here, a piece of that, an extra portion of something else. How can we do it? We only finished lunch just over an hour ago! The people queuing on the stairs at the main entrance to the Restaurant who avoided the tour of the Galley, look down on us with envy, kept in their places by the Restaurant Manager.

"Don't eat it all," someone shouts.

"Leave some for us!"

We are at the Chocoholics Buffet, held once every voyage on P&O ships and several other cruise lines. Everything in front of us is made of chocolate, or at least contains chocolate – with the exception of the hot bread and butter pudding, that is until you smother it with hot chocolate sauce.

I pick up a single truffle and watch as it rolls around and tours my empty plate searching for a friend. I add a small piece of alcoholic chocolate sponge with a blob of whipped cream glistening on top to ensure sufficient calorific intake, and finally a piece of coconut bar dipped in dark chocolate. Himself, as usual enjoying his siesta, likes coconut.

Everywhere around us the tables are already occupied by people eating chocolate – plates full of the stuff, the smell obscures my senses – thoughts of a zoo invade my mind, but I can't think why! Chimpanzees' tea parties, podgy hands stuffing eager mouths, children asking for more. Is that a dolphin's face at the window? The whale is over there – she obviously made it, this afternoon she's wearing a voluminous purple beach cover-up. Hyenas are squabbling, wild boars lowering their heads are searching for empty tables, and huge grizzly bears are licking their paws.

"You've got more than me," one growls to another.

And everywhere the waiters are standing, eager to

assist any passenger with walking difficulties who might not be able to carry their plate piled high with goodies – or indeed any mobile passenger incapable of carrying their over-full plate!

A piece falls on the floor and a child immediately darts to retrieve it.

"We've got to hurry," says its mother. "Dinner starts at 18.30."

I feel vaguely sick with the smell of chocolate as the three of us return to our cabins – my waistband is already tight.

Once in the suite, I carefully cut my three small items into halves, not quite using a ruler, but almost. I want to share them with Himself who is still sound asleep. But I can't bring myself to eat anything.

There's a ring at the door and in walks Satya, a grin on his face, and proudly holding a plate of truffles covered with cling film.

"Just in case you didn't go to the chocoholics buffet Ma'am," he adds as he places the offending objects on the table.

"I knew your husband would be asleep. Maybe he will enjoy them when he wakes."

I try to show real enthusiasm, and thank him as he leaves the room and goes to greet the people in the suite next door with his brilliant smile and calorific offering.

* * * * *

Gone to Jumping Jacks I write on a piece of paper and silently place it on Himself's bedside table. *Back in time for Cocktails!*

We don't have them any longer. You may not either, but if you do, you'll want to know just what is available on board for them. We are talking the C word... C is for Children. Skip the next bit if, like us, you're past it and nappy changing is a dim memory from the distant past, but if you're a generous grandparent, bear it in mind for the future!

How I wish we'd found cruising when our sons were young. It would have been an absolutely perfect kind of holiday for them both.

When Himself and I married, I inherited a 14 year old who had lost his mother to cancer, whereas Himself took on the responsibility for my then 20 month old son from my late husband. What a dreadful mixture to take anywhere, let alone on holiday.

Andrew was a teenager and wanted to *do* things... what, of course, he didn't really know, and when he did eventually get to *do something*, invariably it wasn't what he'd envisaged in the first place. He was a Class A nightmare! – A stands for Adolescent!

John, on the other hand, was an equally difficult problem, a Class B nightmare! – B stands for Baby of course!

By the time we risked a holiday together, the four of us, the new family unit, John was just over two years old and still needing constant attention, meals at awkward times to the rest of us, he ate sparsely of anything that didn't resemble a fish finger, a bread roll or a piece of cheese, was still having a sleep in the afternoon and, thankfully, was in bed early every evening.

"Muuuuum! This milk isn't like we get at home!"

"Muuuuum! This red jam's got bits in it!"

"Muuuuum! I want orange juice without bits in!"

We had bad humour, tantrums, sulks and tears, although thankfully only John had the tears! Add to all that, Himself and I were newly married of course, and really only wanted to be alone – there was little chance.

At the end of *each* holiday, as both the boys steadily grew older, I threatened *never again!* The only redeeming factor in the equation was that the boys 'clicked' from the moment they met and it was terribly sweet to see the 14 year old being followed by the toddler – although I'm not sure that Andrew thought it was sweet – or sitting together watching something, probably quite unsuitable, on the television. At least they were quiet.

How I wish I had found cruising at that stage of their lives.

In the school holiday times, cruise ships are totally heavenly for little people. On board *Aurora* the Toy Box for the under fives is fully supervised, and anyone venturing near the door at the start or finish of a session, is liable to be knocked down in the stampede of happy little children, sometimes with painted faces, or carrying some precious item they've made, and invariably the tears are of those children being collected by their parents.

"I don't want any dinner. I just want to stay here and play!" being the normal cries.

Between six and nine, they progress to Jumping Jacks. The Quarter Deck, a den and disco, is for the ten to 13 year olds and Decibels for the 14 to 17 year olds – you can use your imagination as to what goes on in there, but the loud speakers are huge. If you add to that their own pool and play area on deck, plus Intergalactica, full of computer games for all the family, where you may have to wait in turn behind a Dad for your go on a computer, there really is no reason to hear that dreaded shout of 'Muuum – *I'm bored!*'

And we'll *whisper* the next bit so as not to wake

anybody up – the best bit of all – the night nursery. P&O offers an early dinner and babysitting in a special Night Nursery for the little ones. So go on Mum and Dad, enjoy your dinner in peace and collect any little people when you're ready for bed yourselves.

* * * * *

A couple of years ago Himself and I took his older son and our daughter-in-law on a two week cruise to the Mediterranean in August on the old *Arcadia* (now renamed *Ocean Village*) – something we would normally have avoided as we find the sun in August is too hot for oldies like us.

The reason for the timing of this cruise was young Sam. Aged 11 and an only child, we had promised him the best holiday he'd ever had – and several years later, he's still talking about it. We hardly saw him. At times we wondered if he was still on board. He was organised from morning to night and had a whale of a time.

That was a Football Theme Cruise, which he thoroughly enjoyed, but thankfully we four adults didn't see a single football the whole of the fortnight. I have absolutely no doubt that Sam ate chips and tomato ketchup for every meal, probably including breakfast, he certainly made lots of friends of a similar age, we occasionally caught sight of him doing some organised activity, and he fell into bed each night utterly exhausted.

Given my time again, I know where I'd be taking Andrew and John for their holidays. Thankfully they are both now adults, but I have warned them that when I get old (really old!), all I want is for them to book me onto a world cruise each and every January! What bliss!

* * * * *

Back to reality – I can forget all that, until I become a grandmother, a long time in the future!

"Come on Darling. We have to get changed," I gently nudge Himself out of his siesta mode.

"More cocktails tonight. We should get organised."

* * * * *

Our last cocktail party, but tonight it's a special one. The invitation reads :

Staff Captain David Box
requests the pleasure of your company...

us! Held in the Uganda Room on Deck 13, just behind the huge Crow's Nest at the front of the ship, and with delicious canapés, it is a very select gathering and we're privileged to be here.

Whilst I was chatting to other people, Himself had a long conversation with David Box.

"He's leaving the ship at Southampton for two and a half months' holiday," he told me later. "Guess what he's doing?"

I hate those kinds of questions... trekking through the Sahara? Prospecting for gold in America? Deep sea diving? Training to be an astronaut? I'd run out of ideas.

"He and his wife are going sailing by themselves in their own boat for two and a half months!"

"Isn't that a sort of busman's holiday?" I laughed. But Himself can't remember where he said they were going... he possibly wasn't told... after all, the last thing Mrs David Box would appreciate seeing would be a huge

P&O ship on the horizon bearing down upon their seclusion. So wherever it was, we hope you both had calm seas and plenty of peace and quiet.

Bing Bong! "Good evening Ladies and Gentlemen. Dinner is now being served in the Alexandria and Medina Restaurants. Do have a *yummy* evening on board *Aurora.*"

(OK. So can you think of a better word beginning with 'y'? After all, you have been to the Chocoholics buffet today.)

"Not another dinner! I'm beginning to look forward to some Beans on Toast!"

The look on his face showed that Himself didn't agree with my choice of food, but he knew what I meant. There really does come a time when something simple would be perfect.

And on the entertainment goes... a Maritime Lecture with Peter Boyd-Smith, today talking about Cunard from 1840 to the present day, including the *Lusitania, Mauritania* and the *Queens.* You could have enjoyed an Indian Head Massage at 15.00 or watched the Children's Fancy Dress Competition. If you're Jewish, you could celebrate the Jewish Sabbath at 17.30 in the Uganda Room. Why not watch P&O's presentation this evening called Homeward Bound or what about attending Astronomy for Beginners at 23.30 outside the Crow's Nest on Deck 13?

Or just let's take a Bounty Hunter, today's Cocktail of the Day, made of Bacardi rum, Crème de Cacao, coconut and cream, and sip it quietly in a comfortable seat on Promenade Deck and watch the sea go past, followed by a 'zzzzzzzzzzzzzzzzz' evening on board!

16

PACKING

In the event, we had a *zestful* evening last night, and today it's Saturday. If you look out of the nearest window or porthole, you'll see nothing but sea! We are in the Bay of Biscay where we'll be until mid-afternoon and then we'll head towards our home port of Southampton through the Western Approaches to the English Channel.

As is normally the case, the Bay is being kind and doesn't interrupt us, as virtually everyone on board is now intent on repacking luggage. What a horrid job, and one that puts a damper on the atmosphere on board.

"Have you packed yet?" will be the favourite question at lunch.

Most will be pleased, and relieved, to admit, "Virtually everything," but there will be those who take pleasure in announcing "I'll do mine after the show this evening!"

Luggage. Do you remember that beautifully packed case you brought on? That hanging wardrobe which contained your evening clothes, the small suitcase full of essentials for the cruise? Himself always takes Ginger Marmalade! I think it's an age thing! Of course P&O provides perfectly adequate jams and marmalades, but two weeks without a bit of Ginger has him pining for home, and after several irritable mutterings about *little pots of jam*, I've found it so much easier just to pack a jar.

At this point I'll whisper *McVities Dark Chocolate biscuits* – nothing on board is quite so delicious for nibbling on the balcony with the afternoon cuppa – but don't advertise the fact, or I'll have a long queue at our door on the next cruise.

But back to the packing! Of course packing to come home is easy – or it should be! Everything in your cabin that is not owned by P&O has to be removed and hopefully packed into your suitcases. Did I mention earlier that you can take as much luggage on board as you feel you need – in my case these days that almost includes the kitchen sink, although I did find the taps very awkward to pack for this trip. The only limitation is how you get it to the ship, and, of course, how you store it whilst you are on board. Cabins range in size from adequate to large, depending on how much you're prepared to pay for your accommodation, and on which ship you have decided to travel. Empty suitcases can be stored under your bed until needed, often the smaller one disappearing into the larger one. Any item too large to be pushed out of sight can be removed by your steward and stored elsewhere for the duration of the voyage, although we have never found this option necessary.

* * * * *

But before we start our packing, we have something very

important to enjoy. There's a ring at the bell, and in walks Satya, preceded by balloons and laden with goodies.

"Good morning Sir. Happy Birthday," he beams as he starts to lay the table.

Today is Himself's birthday – a pause whilst I sing *Happy Birthday to Himseeeelf,* totally out of tune as usual.

We are about to enjoy a Champagne Breakfast.

Our normal breakfast of cereals and fruit has been replaced by a wondrous assortment of cold meats and paté, cheese and fruit, rolls and croissants, freshly brewed coffee and a bottle of bubbly. We'll leave the chocolates until later.

"Not bad for a snack," Himself grins.

"What happened to that '*I'm not hungry*' comment you made a moment ago?" I ask.

"Pop!" the cork bounces out of the bottle and Satya pours out two glasses of the bubbling liquid.

"What a pity we're home tomorrow," Himself says. "It would have been so much nicer to be able to *really* relax and *really* enjoy this breakfast… in bed."

I frown at him, knowing what he has in mind.

"Breakfast and then packing," I grin at Satya, who leaves, having put the champagne bottle into the ice bucket. "Let's concentrate on the matter in hand Darling, and see how much time we've left when we've finished!"

"That's exactly what I thought we'd do," he raises his eyebrows.

"The packing, my dear… the packing! Let's get the packing done first!"

"Spoil sport! It *is* my birthday!"

During breakfast I push the button on the television.

"What have you put that on for?" Himself asks. "We

never watch television at breakfast!" he adds, spooning some Ginger Marmalade onto a warm croissant and making me go "Yuck!"

"Thought I'd see what's going on today on board!" I pass the comment casually.

"What? On our last day? Obviously the sun's got to you."

"There!" I yell. "Look!" pointing at the television. "It's for you! A message for you!"

And there on the screen appears a birthday cake complete with lighted candles and the message HAPPY BIRTHDAY HIMSELF FROM JEAN AND TERRY, our Jack Nicholson look alike and his wife. We hum along to the Happy Birthday tune which now fills our cabin.

"Wasn't that nice of them." Himself smiles. "Did you know about it?"

And he laughs at my raised eyebrow!

* * * * *

It is probably best to draw a veil over the next hour or so – it was, after all, Himself's birthday.

Back to the horrid subject of packing.

It's about now that you realise you have a problem. Nature being what it is, we invariably pack a suitcase to its full capacity.

"I'll just put that in – it might be useful and I do have the space."

"What about your pink floaty top?"

"Well it wouldn't take much space… "

So I add that, but of course I'll need my pink shoes… and on it goes.

Do you remember buying that handbag in Florence, and the one in Barcelona? The skirt in the shop on board, the beach bag in Gibraltar, and the face creams there? And what about that huge beach towel that was such a bargain and attracted you both – so much so that you bought a second, and then one for your son at home, and that pashmina for your sister and... but I needn't go on. I'm sure you've got the picture. And don't forget you have to pack all those gifts you picked up in Egypt too!

Each item may be quite easy to handle individually, but en masse they have created your problem.

P&O has the answer – it's obviously met this situation once or twice before. So off you go to the shops on board and buy one, or two, of their blue canvas collapsible holdalls with the name of the ship printed on the side. They're absolutely perfect for accommodating all those bulky light items which you've been collecting around the Mediterranean. And not only that, when you get home, you can collapse it and put it into your suitcase so it's ready for your next cruise – well there will be one, won't there?

One of the joys of cruising, especially with companies like P&O, Cunard and Fred. Olsen who sail from the UK, is the lack of effort involved with your luggage. You pack it and unpack it, but they move it. It doesn't matter if you're 28 or 82, just pack your suitcases, lock them, label them, put them outside your cabin door from where, as if by magic, they all disappear – until they're reclaimed by you in the luggage hall tomorrow morning in Southampton.

But we've jumped ahead of ourselves. Before sending off everything except what you're wearing, which will disappear until tomorrow, you ought to decide what you are going to wear tonight... and what you want to travel home in!

The last night on board is always casual dress and a lot of people go to dinner tonight in the clothes they will travel home in. I know a lady who had red wine spilled down her front at dinner on the last night of her cruise, but had to wear the stained top the following day as her suitcases had long since disappeared into the bowels of the ship. She now keeps a spare top – just in case.

Himself and I put most of our luggage outside the cabin door before we go to dinner, but keep one bag back until we are ready to go to bed, which covers accidents with food or wine, but also helps the staff as the heavy luggage is removed early in the evening.

It is up to you, but any luggage you are not intending to carry off the ship yourself, without any help from the crew, must be outside your cabin before you finally go to bed. There are, of course, always plenty of staff around to help any disabled passengers.

Most passengers these days have a small suitcase, usually on wheels, into which tomorrow morning they pack their night-clothes, sponge bags, and anything fragile. Of course always keep any medication with you, because once a suitcase has been removed from outside your door, it is virtually impossible to retrieve it. I have never seen the luggage stored 'below stairs' ready for disembarkation, but if every passenger on this ship only had one suitcase each, there would be a minimum of 1,800.

Cruise passengers don't often adopt a travel light attitude to holiday wardrobes, unless an air flight is involved.

* * * * *

So we've done the bulk of our packing and the next job on the list is a sticky one. Tipping. I hate it. I'd far rather the cruise companies included it in the cost of the cruise, and then paid their staff directly... but most of them don't, and Himself mutters: "they probably wouldn't get it all – the company would keep some."

Whatever – tipping is part of cruising.

In P&O's folder in your cabin, you'll find a very helpful leaflet which explains just who you should tip and the basic amount per person. Obviously your room steward, the guy who has kept your cabin clean and tidy during the cruise and with whom you are probably now on very friendly terms, he deserves his tips.

Then there are the two waiters in the dining room who have remembered each night that you only drink black decaffeinated coffee after dinner, never eat white bread, but like plenty of vegetables. They've been wonderful, friendly, helpful and seen that your trousers now no longer fit. They are not responsible for the calorific intake of your food – you chose from the menus they gave you... but I bet you never received the wrong dish... and bear in mind that English is usually not their native language. They certainly deserve their tips too.

The wine waiters who have been the cause of a hangover or two are usually not tipped, as they are paid a percentage from all the drinks they sell – although if one has been particularly attentive, it might be nice to tip him or her, but that is your choice.

A tip to the Head Waiter and/or his or her assistant, and if you've had a lot of room service, it would be nice to tip this guy too. We've been regular diners in Café Bordeaux and we'll certainly put some money into the collection box there for the waiters, but we've only eaten a couple of times in the Orangery, so we'll give that collection box a miss.

And when do you do it? Tips for your room steward and dining room waiters are usually placed in small envelopes, obtainable from Reception, and handed to the steward as you leave your cabin for dinner tonight, and to the waiters at the end of the meal. There will be much hugging and hand shaking as waiters and passengers exchange thanks, and your table-mates, now new friends, part, often having exchanged addresses.

* * * * *

But life carries on as usual on board. This may be our last day, but we don't want to waste a moment of our luxury cruise. So, having packed, leave the suitcases where they are and let's go and find the action.

There was something in the Gym called Tummy Toner at 09.00, but thankfully we've missed that, and anyway, mine is well past that stage. If you hurry, you'll be in time for the Handicapped Longest Drive Competition in the Golf Simulator on Deck 13. A quiz called 'Name that Tune', a dance class to learn the Salsa, friendly Bridge, (have you seen how fierce some of the Bridge players can be?) Deck Quoits, Shuffleboard and Cricket – you mean you haven't found the Sports Nets on Deck 13?

I shall attend a lecture, using the word loosely, called Pre-Flight Feet, which hopefully will show me how to prevent swollen feet and ankles on long journeys.

Himself is going to another Maritime lecture given by Peter Boyd-Smith about transportation by road, sea, rail and air – including vintage motoring, steam trains, sailing ships, airships and airliners. That should keep him happy for an hour or so – excuse me whilst I yawn!

The children are not forgotten, although we've not seen much of any of them during the cruise, they have been on board the whole time! Occasionally we caught sight of a happy face, sometimes carrying a newly created masterpiece, or briefly chatting to parents before rushing off to their next organised activity. Today there's a Children's Talent Show, so if you have a budding Shirley Temple, bring her along – this could be her lucky day. And at 19.30 there's a Madhatter's Tea Party in the Toybox on Deck eight.

Have you started thinking nautically yet? Will you go into the galley to make dinner tomorrow evening, and to the deck above to your cabin when it's time for bed? Life will seem very flat tomorrow evening – especially if, like me, you'll be knee deep in piles of laundry.

* * * * *

But there's an activity I haven't mentioned because I rarely play, although today I might make an exception. Bingo! Every day at sea at 16.00 ladies *and* gentlemen have been seen heading towards Carmen's, eagerly hoping to win the jackpot and recoup some of the money they've spent during the cruise. But there are two sorts of Bingo players... those who go along religiously every day, and those who, knowing the jackpot must be won today, suddenly get the urge to play – sorry folks! I'm one of those. Hopefully whoever wins today will be a regular player – after all, they're the ones who have contributed to the jackpot which has steadily been increasing during the cruise and now stands at a magnificent £1,300 – but there is something called beginner's luck!

Some years ago on a Royal Caribbean cruise ship we joined four friends and visited the Baltic Capitals and on the last day before we returned to Harwich, the six of us at our dinner table decided to play Bingo, pooling any winnings! As if we should be so lucky! In the dining room at the table next to us sat a couple we'd all met on a cruise to North Cape and the fjords on the same ship the previous year. They too had the same idea.

"Two fat ladies – 88."

"On its own, number 3."

"Sweet 16."

"Doctor's Orders, number 9."

"All the sixes, 66."

We didn't win – but we knew someone who did. The lady from the table next to us – we'll call her Mary – and guess what, that night at dinner she treated the whole of the table to one bottle of imitation champagne – between eight!... and she'd won nearly £2,000. In the unlikely event of me ever winning that sort of money, my table companions would have had a hangover for at least a week!

But back to today – the packing is done, the tipping is organised, and having reached 'z' last night, we're now enjoying an *amorous* or *brilliant* evening on board *Aurora*.

We're now at dinner for our last evening meal, and there are balloons floating above our table – think back to this morning's celebration breakfast!

Dinner is, as normal, delicious food, wonderful desserts, freely flowing conversation, and then they all gather... all the waiters from our area of the dining room accompanied by the Head Waiter. A cake with one candle alight is placed in front of Himself.

"There isn't room for the full number of candles," I

grin at him, as the waiter's choir breaks into chorus.

"Happy birthday to you," – clap, clap, clap.

"Happy birthday to you," – clap, clap, clap.

"Happy Birthday dear Himself," – clap, clap, clap,

"Happy Birthday to yoooooooooooou." More clapping, which gives the whole rendition a feeling of Caribbean flavour, and one of the waiters then pops all the balloons, which explode with loud bangs to the applause of everyone from the tables around.

But did we really want cake on top of our dinner and dessert?

* * * * *

Following our final show, it's time for bed. Firstly we put out our final suitcase. Secondly we eat our final chocolates, which have been placed on our pillows each night by our room steward, and finally, leaving the safe passage of *Aurora* to Captain Walters and his crew, we fall asleep for the final time in our wonderful cabin.

17

SOUTHAMPTON

Returning to Southampton always fills me with a mixture of feelings – at least today, towards the end of May, the sun is shining brightly and the warmth is already being felt through the doors to our balcony.

"I'll soon have the washing dry," I think aloud.

Of course I love getting home to the mountain of mail that always awaits, to the long list of messages from the couple who look after our home and Tom, our ancient feline friend, whilst we're away, and of course to seeing Tom himself again.

Balanced against all that is my love of travel, of visiting new places, learning about the way different people live and the endless hours I have free for writing.

There are few calls upon my time on board ship. Himself never calls upstairs to me: "Do you want a cup of tea Darling?" – which roughly translated means 'I'd love a cup of tea Darling'. Neither do I get persistent plaintiff meows to remind me that it's past his lunch or dinner time from Tom, who seems to prefer my lap best when I'm trying to use my computer keyboard!

Sitting on the balcony I am undisturbed and can really concentrate... except for the constant need to look out to sea in case I am missing some sea creatures going about their daily routine.

Here in Southampton there is no chance of seeing a whale, but I'll just have a quick look over the side for the last time to ensure that Captain Walters has tied *Aurora* up safely alongside the quay. We hope he'll have some passengers on board on the next cruise who will keep an eye out for him. It must be a comforting thought for him to know that we passengers are looking after *him*. P&O really ought to issue regular cruisers with log books! It's been a pleasure to spend a fortnight with this excellent Captain, with whom we have sailed many times before.

"Have you sailed into Venice?"
"Do you remember the sights as we approached Malta?"
"Can't wait to visit Istanbul again... "

As a port, Southampton will never be listed amongst the prettiest. I am looking out over row upon row of warehouse roofs, car parks and factories – as far as the eye can see. No wonderful mountains beyond. No ancient fortifications to tempt the eager sightseer. No vaparettos and gondolas floating past. Southampton is not a place you'd rush to visit again, although for any of the crew who are able to have a few hours off the ship, it is good for shopping... but wait! What's that? The spire of a very pretty church to the left... possibly worth a visit!

It's 07.30 and Himself and I are fully dressed, much to the amazement of ourselves as well as Satya, who has popped in briefly to say goodbye. I stop gazing down at the hive of industry to say goodbye to this delightful young man who has helped to make our holiday superbly comfortable and who will later today board an aircraft for his flight home – it is monsoon time in Mumbai (Bombay) – he can't wait to return to his next ship in three months' time.

As Satya leaves our suite, I quickly organise breakfast. On most ships there is no room service on the last morning as all the staff are involved elsewhere, but a little forward planning and a quick visit to the Orangery yesterday morning has solved the problem. We each have a bowl of cereal and with the remains of our fruit bowl contents we enjoy our breakfast. Neither of us is a morning person and neither of us can face either a trip to the Restaurant or a visit to the Orangery.

We sit quietly, me still munching my muesli, totally oblivious to the frantic activity going on the other side of our cabin door.

"Have you emptied the safe?" I ask between mouthfuls.

"Mmmm," Himself nods in confirmation.

"Returned your library book?"

"Mmmm," Himself nods again in mid-mouthful.

"Filled in the Questionnaire?"

"Mmmm!"

He's getting irritated, so I concentrate on trapping the last of my muesli, which is now attempting circuits of my cereal bowl.

Disembarkation day is always hectic. Not only do all 1,800 of we passengers have to leave *Aurora*, collect our luggage and make our way home, but also the ship has to be prepared for the 1,800 new passengers who are, at this moment, making their way to the Mayflower Terminal from all directions in the UK and sometimes from abroad.

There are some lucky passengers who will be staying

on board and enjoying *Aurora's* next cruise to Spain, Portugal, Canary Islands, Madeira and France lasting ten nights. This is known as a 'back to back' cruise and often there are wonderful reductions available for passengers wishing to stay float. Sadly the majority of us have to return to the real world and say goodbye to our luxury floating hotel, which has been our very comfortable home for the last fortnight.

Down below on the quayside the workforce has been in action since the moment the ship was cleared by the port authorities. From my vantage point high on the side of the ship, I am unable to see the frantic effort going on inside the bowels of *Aurora*, where all our baggage is being moved into position to be off-loaded onto the quay. Once off the ship, it is placed in the huge hanger-like Baggage Hall in deck order, and colour coded according to where your cabin has been on *Aurora* and your method of onward transportation. As yet no passengers are allowed to leave *Aurora*.

"Bing Bong... Would the following passengers please contact Reception immediately:

Mr Blank of Cabin A123.

Mrs West of Cabin C345.

Mr and Mrs North of Cabin D654.

And Mr and Mrs Smith of Cabin E531."

On every trip, it is the same – there are passengers who have not paid their on-board accounts, and of course, until they do, no one will be allowed ashore.

The easiest way to ensure your account is cleared is to register your credit card at Reception well in advance of our arrival back at Southampton. It is also possible to clear the balance in cash, travellers' cheques, or even by cheque if you have made arrangements beforehand to do this.

Some ten minutes later: "Bing Bong... Will the following passenger please contact Reception immediately.

Mr Blank of Cabin A123."

Still one passenger remains elusive.

By now, despite repeated requests over the ship's address system not to block Reception areas and to remain in the comfort of the public lounges, Deck 5 is heaving with passengers, making transit of this central area very difficult.

"Bing Bong... Will Mr Blank of Cabin A123 *please* contact Reception by calling from the nearest telephone as soon as possible."

This is the last time we hear Mr Blank's name, so we assume his account has been settled.

On the quayside the stores for the next cruise are being loaded towards the rear of the ship, whilst even more are being deposited by orange fork lift trucks in the space they leave. Loo rolls and lettuces, flowers and fruit, alcohol and aspirins. Everything needed to cater for 1,800 passengers and 850 crew on a ten day cruise which leaves at 17.00 this afternoon.

Sitting here quietly in our bare suite, now cleared of all our personal belongings, we await the announcement which tells holders of our colour of Gangway Pass to gather together all our belongings and leave *Aurora* via the exit on Deck 5 near Reception.

When travelling with P&O, two days before disembarkation, coloured luggage labels and matching coloured Gangway Passes will be delivered to your cabin. If you need more labels, contact Reception at this time. Every item of luggage which is put outside your door for removal the night before Southampton must have a coloured luggage label. It is this label which determines where your luggage is placed in the luggage hall.

I know this *is* very boring, but it is essential information. After all, you'd hate your suitcases full of dirty washing to evade your immediate attention on arrival back home, wouldn't you? Worse still, you might lose those genuine imitation ancient scarab beetles, the Pharaoh's death mask you so loved and the paintings on papyrus you collected on your Nile trip – it was just as well there was no weight limitation on my magic carpet!

Hold on to the coloured card as you will need this to disembark, once all the luggage has left the ship and has been sorted into order in the luggage hall.

So now, whilst Himself reads his first few pages of today's Daily Telegraph – some newspapers are now on sale in one of the lounges – I have a few loose ends to tie up for you.

Firstly, congratulations to Mr Jones of Cabin F178 who came closest to guessing the weight of the *White Sister's* cake, which was 75lbs 11oz. Mr Jones was only one ounce out. Well done! I hope you enjoyed your prize of a bottle of 'bubbly'.

Secondly, Harold and his harem! Do you remember at the end of Chapter four I mentioned Harold? And since then I haven't said a word about him – but I have caught sight of him around the ship, although I've never actually *seen* him, if you know what I mean – it's best to let sleeping dogs lie!

He was on a cruise Himself and I did a few years ago – and his name wasn't Harold. Himself and I joined *his* table. I say *his* table because that's what it felt like. He was accompanied by, and presided over, his harem – again the names are changed.

There was Theresa, a buxom blonde from way across the water who liked more than a drop or two of the Liffy water – almost intravenously and apparently with little residual effect the following day. Belinda-Jo who had been Queen Bee of *somewhere's* WI and went on and on, and on... and on... and on about it – and then went on again – really yawn provoking stuff. Heather who was soft and gentle and would never have said 'Boo' to a goose, had such a bird been on board, and who was quite swamped by the rest of the harem. And dear Kay, a truly delightful octogenarian with the heart and mind of a 50 year old, with whom we have kept in touch in the intervening years.

Oh... and Harold... we mustn't forget Harold – that wouldn't please him at all. In his 70s then, he'd obviously been a handsome man in his day, but how he managed to gather together such an assorted harem, I'll never quite understand.

And did I mention that Belinda-Jo had been Queen Bee of somewhere's WI? I'm sure you've got the picture.

Do you remember me saying it's very unusual to find yourself on a table where you just cannot get on with your table companions, and that basically most people who cruise are very friendly and often amusing? This table was our one exception in all the time Himself and I have been afloat.

"Contact the Restaurant Manager and ask to change tables," would be my advice on finding yourself in this unfortunate situation, and sooner rather than later too. How I wish someone had given me that advice years ago.

It was the last trip of the *Canberra,* a ship loved by many but to us, new to cruising and new to her, she seemed to be held together by paint and prayers.

"Best place for her," was our reaction when we heard she was to be scrapped, although even on this cruise over the past couple of weeks on *Aurora* where the ship is very modern, I have heard apparently perfectly nice, sane and intelligent people praising *Canberra* and regretting her passing.

"I'm going to ask to change tables," Himself told me after a particularly difficult meal when Harold had been more than usually unpleasant.

"Please don't," I had begged him. I'm the lady who dislikes making a fuss over anything.

"We're halfway through the cruise, and he probably won't be so bad tomorrow."

But he was, and he got worse still instead of better, and every meal became an ordeal to be got through. I dreaded dinner time, but I dreaded lunch time even more as, undiluted by his harem's company, Harold would home in on us all by himself, wherever we were, and there was no escape. I'm sure he lay in wait behind pot plants, ready to ambush us. Only breakfast was OK. Harold didn't do breakfast. He was obviously recovering from the night before.

This sad state continued until six days before the end of the cruise when Himself walked into our tiny cabin, beaming from ear to ear.

"We've changed tables," he grinned, "and not only that, but we're changing restaurants too!"

What joy! What bliss! Why didn't I let him do it before? From here on in, meals were a delight and something to be anticipated with joy.

And Harold? We never saw him again. I thought he'd jumped ship, or even gone to join that huge cruise club in the sky – that is until this cruise... but as I didn't actually get to shake his hand, maybe he was a ghost!

"Did you see Harold?" I asked Himself.

"Why are you giving me that odd look? You **do** believe I saw him – don't you?"

Remember, your cruise is *your* holiday, as well as everyone else's on board – why dread meal times? Why spoil a major part of cruising, as meal times tend to be? A quiet request to the Restaurant Manager can invariably secure a change in the seating arrangements. I certainly wish I'd not stopped Himself from asking for the change of table. Life is too short to tolerate unpleasant, argumentative people – even if they do have their own harem.

And thirdly, *Pollywogs and Shellbacks Afloat* – the title of this book. Strange names. But wait a moment – I'll have to tell you later. There is the announcement we've been waiting for.

"Bing Bong! Ladies and Gentlemen. All the baggage is now in the Baggage Hall and awaiting collection. At this time, will all passengers holding a Gold coloured Gangway Pass please leave the ship, ensuring they take all personal possessions with them."

"Come on," Himself hurries me. "That's us! Let's go!"

* * * * *

Tom is happy – he'd purr if he could, but thyroid problems have prevented this in his old age. But he's obviously happy that we're back home as he curls up next to me as Himself and I start on the mountain of mail. We sort them into three piles. Junk mail for the bin, interesting mail to be dealt with immediately and, of course, cruise offers.

"I see they're still offering our trip to Iceland," Himself says. "And our *QE2* trip at the end of the year."

We've been away just a fortnight and in that time several tempting offers of interesting cruises have dropped through our letter box.

And what do I find when I check my email? One from Mr and Mrs F.T.C. that says they've just booked a world cruise leaving next January.

"What took you so long?" I reply – there's no need to ask if they've enjoyed their first cruise.

* * * * *

The morning after the fortnight before!

"What's the matter?" Himself looks concerned at hearing my groan.

"Aaaah. I see! Bad news eh?"

His face changes from concern to amusement as he sees me scowling down at the bathroom scales, whilst trying to hold in the extra stomach I seem to have collected en route.

"It's probably water retention!" he tries to console me.

"It probably isn't!"

"Why don't you ask P&O to start a Slimming Club on board?"

He narrowly avoids the wet loofah.

And finally, *Pollywogs and Shellbacks Afloat.* When crossing the Equator on board a Cunard Ship, His Imperial Majesty, Neptune of the Deep, accompanied by His Queen and Seaweed Court grace the vessel with their presence and summons all Pollywogs and Shellbacks to attend the ceremony. Shellbacks are passengers who have crossed the Equator on board ship before. Pollywogs have not – and often end up in the swimming pool!

18

DE-STRESSING
IN ONE EASY LESSON

High on a list of stressful events you may be surprised to find the word 'holiday' alongside bereavement, marriage, house move and losing your job.

Stressful? Are the people compiling such lists talking about the planning or the actual holiday, or even the aftermath when the holidaymaker desperately tries to pull scattered brains back into the real world?

Yes I can accept that climbing Everest would definitely be stressful to an office worker, or that a cold, wet week incarcerated in a caravan with two screaming children would hardly be classed as restful. If he's normally used to catching the 07.30 to Waterloo this would indeed be enough to drive any husband to experience unacceptable levels of stress – not to mention the trauma caused to his poor wife having to supply meals from a strange and often minute kitchen and entertain less than enthusiastic offspring whose boredom threshold is directly related to the weather forecast.

Holidays are meant to be enjoyable and beneficial – a rest, a change, a period of recreational time spent away from work, study or general routine. Twenty-four hours of rain thundering on a caravan roof does not bring to mind the Americanism R and R, or even rest and recuperation. After a holiday you are supposed to feel refreshed, renewed and ready to resume your normal life with vigour and enthusiasm.

There is, of course, an enormous assortment of holidays to suit all age groups which also take into consideration different sized budgets. What suits you when you're a teenager or young adult may well be quite unacceptable when you're in receipt of your free bus pass.

However, I am delighted to inform all those of you about to embark on the annual stressful occupation of deciding which mountain to climb this year, that there is an alternative. Or maybe you would prefer to enjoy the rain thundering onto your caravan, or even spending two days of your precious holiday allowance checking in your baggage at a crowded airport, followed by suffering jet lag or Delhi Belly caught in India, or Montezuma's Revenge caught anywhere else, or just even spending four days recovering from the cold caught in mid-flight, courtesy of some unhealthy passenger who happened to be airborne with you.

Having read this book, how do you fancy a luxury cruise? What? Never thought about one before! Do you consider yourself to be far too young, far too old, too infirm, disabled, got small children, vegetarian, Buddhist, member of Alcoholics Anonymous, golfer, Bridge fanatic, Line Dancer extraordinaire or would you just like somewhere to sit quietly and read and have your meals served beautifully without having to contemplate the washing up? Well, now you know you can be all of these, and do all of that on a cruise, and loads more as well, so now, how would YOU fancy a cruise?

Of course you would. But would you like to know how to get it right the first time – unlike us? The first cruise my husband and I took was years ago, and if we were choosing it today, knowing what we now know, we'd end up with a much better deal. That first cruise cost a lot of money and far more than we needed to pay. So, for your benefit I'm going to wind the clock back and show you how to go about it, so that with confidence you can choose and book your cruise, obtain the best value for your money and get it spot on at your first attempt.

* * * * *

Where would you like to go?

A simple question, though not as easy as it first seems, although of course you may be one of the few who have always had an urge to visit a specific destination. Even so, most of that which follows will still be of interest. Picking a cruise is like opening a large box of expensive chocolates. Have one and you'll want to try them all. You are spoilt for choice and can't see the wood for the trees – or even the ships for the seas. So to begin with, off you go to your nearest Travel Agents and collect your first armful of brochures, no doubt the first of many – and start a pile of them in *your* sitting room, like we have in ours... eventually you too will update this pile each year, and eventually you too will sadly throw out the old brochures which will have become old friends, before the pile threatens to topple over.

Open a cruise brochure and you'll soon be transported by the pictures to endless exotic destinations. Although I am an internet user, this is one occasion where the brochure is much more satisfying. Nothing beats sitting in front of a roaring fire in the middle of a bitterly cold winter's evening, glass of wine, lager or gin and tonic in hand, turning the pages of the brochures and allowing the sunshine to tumble out into your home.

We have all seen pictures of people in advertisements standing on the deck of a ship, hand in hand, holding onto the rail, and gazing out to the wide blue yonder. Well, it is now time to imagine yourself in that situation.

For the next week you can happily flick through these brochures and obtain a brief overview of the cruising world – for world indeed it is. Virtually any country that has a coastline can be a cruise ship destination, and several cities away from the coast can also be visited by river cruises.

The first thing you will notice is there are two main kinds of cruise – Cruises from UK ports and Fly Cruises. Living in the south of England as I do, cruises which we find convenient depart from several places including Southampton, London, Dover and Harwich. By virtue of our position in the world, we are invariably faced with a trip across the Bay of Biscay before we reach warmer climates, except when crossing the Atlantic. Obviously Norway, Iceland and the Baltic Capitals also avoid a Bay crossing.

The words 'Bay of Biscay' often fill the inexperienced cruiser with horror and bring to mind stories of huge waves, rough seas and seasickness. But as you now know, these stories are just not true. I'm sure you've all heard of fishermen's stories, and of *that much* being at least *six inches* – well Bay of Biscay stories can be filed in the same drawer. As I've already said, I have crossed the Bay many times, at all times of the year from February to December and only once have I had a bad crossing. And let's face it, an enforced diet for twenty-four hours at the start of a cruise can be beneficial, as you probably now understand.

The roughest weather I have ever experienced was one balmy September evening, as we were leaving Cannes, in the south of France, when suddenly a dreadful storm blew up out of nowhere. The Captain announced that we should secure all moveable items in our cabins, and the people in the cabin next door ignored his advice. They lost a bottle of spirits which slid the full length of their dressing table before crashing to the floor, narrowly avoiding the wastepaper bin! Warnings of this nature are extremely rare – I suspect that Gordon's have built an anti-tilt mechanism into their gin bottles which enables excessive drinkers, sailors AND cruise passengers to keep their precious contents vertical – even when at times they themselves are not!

Fly Cruises are what they imply – you fly from a UK airport and after some hours in an aeroplane arrive, hopefully somewhere hot, and transfer to your ship a couple of hours or so later. They are great inventions if you are either short of time or wish to explore destinations further afield. Alaska, for example, is difficult as a destination if you can't or won't fly. The disadvantages of Fly Cruising are the time wasted at airports at both ends of the flight (and normally at both ends of the cruise too), the health worries which more and more people have these days about the safety of flying – think SARS and DVTs – and, of course, the weight limitations permitted by the airlines.

Having been told I can pack everything including

the kitchen sink, I invariably do just that. The amount of luggage you can take on a cruise that departs from and returns to a UK port is limited only by the space available in the vehicle in which you travel to that port. Even if you are collected from your home by a coach, and many of the cruise companies have sweeper coaches that collect at various points around the UK, you will still be able to carry more luggage, and if like me you find it difficult to travel light, this is definitely a consideration.

* * * * *

Now, having decided where you want to visit, you may well have noticed from thumbing through your increasing pile of brochures – and by now you've probably realised that cruise brochures are indeed like chocolates and very '*more-ish*' – that several companies visit the same destinations. The dates you have in mind will be a major factor as to which one suits you best, and maybe one cruise visits a certain port you have always wanted to see, whereas another cruise doesn't

These are personal preferences and, of course, only you can decide. You can also try Theme Cruises and also Educational ones. But don't be put off by a Theme Cruise that doesn't interest you, if everything else about the cruise is right. As I've already said, Himself and I didn't see a single football on the Football Theme Cruise we did one summer with a grandchild, but then we didn't actually look for one either. The grandchild thoroughly enjoyed the theme, along with everything else about his cruise, so don't be put off by a Jazz Theme Cruise, if you only like classical music.

And on the subject of grandchildren, cruises are what you want them to be, and basically most cruises suit all sorts of people, young and old. You can do as little as you please, get involved with everything that is offered or quietly go and read in a corner or find somewhere to turn different shades of mahogany.

Facilities on board are excellent for everyone from the youngest baby to the oldest pensioner. Children and teenagers are well catered for, and people on special diets find no problems provided they inform the booking agent at the time they make their booking. Obviously if you intensely dislike anyone under 18, and these people do exist, it would be sensible to avoid a Mediterranean cruise in the middle of August, whereas the Norwegian Fjords don't appear to attract so many youngsters.

Most people with disabilities or medical conditions will find a cruise the ideal sort of holiday. Some of the newer ships have special cabins for the disabled, and most ships have plenty of lifts and always staff on hand to help wheelchair passengers up and down the gangway – and no, let's finish on the correct note, it is not called a gangplank. During my cruises I have frequently watched as wheelchair passengers are transferred from ship to shore without a single problem – even onto the tenders if the ship is at anchor rather than in port.

Tenders? What a large cruising vocabulary you now have. These lifeboats are permanently on display, and every passenger hopes they will never be needed – except to ferry them to and from the ship where the sea is shallow and it is not possible for the ship to tie up at the dockside.

The size of the ship varies widely. A cruise I remember with great pleasure was many years ago on a Geest Banana Boat to the Caribbean from South Wales. There were only 12 passengers on board and virtually no facilities except for adequate, but comfortable, cabins on a 10,000 ton vessel. We were provided with a few videos, Scrabble and Monopoly and some packs of cards. We made our own entertainment and had lots of laughter. The food was delicious, if at times somewhat limited in choice, but knowing how my waist has increased over the years, this probably wasn't a bad thing. The cruise was great fun, but the trip would have been quite hopeless for a family with teenagers, an absolute nightmare for a family with toddlers and out of the question for disabled or elderly people requiring access to medical facilities.

I love long trips with several days at sea when the ship remains out of sight of land. I find them incredibly relaxing, whereas some people I know prefer to visit a different port each day, and I find that quite exhausting.

70,000 tons gives you a large ship with lots of facilities and plenty of space – a good size for a first cruise. 70,000 tons? Can you visualise that? Probably not! I'm sure you've all seen the *Queen Elizabeth 2* either afloat, in newspapers and magazines or on television. She, and for some reason they're always 'she', has a gross tonnage of just over 70,000 tons and the new *Queen Mary 2* will be approximately twice that size! Indeed a floating village.

* * * * *

So, I assume you have now decided on your destination, the dates of your holiday, the ship you want to travel on and are now ready to book your cruise.

A first glance at the prices quoted often doesn't make for pleasant reading. However, do bear in mind that discounts are frequently offered even in the brochure itself, and booking through one of the many cruise clubs now operating is easy, safe and simple and ensures you get the best possible value for your money. These cruise clubs, which frequently advertise in the travel section of the weekend newspapers, do not cost anything to 'join' – you merely ask to be put onto their mailing lists. You can contact more than one cruise club and obtain other quotations.

Don't forget to ask if they have any special offers – often first time cruisers get special deals on newcomers cruises – and do also mention it if you are celebrating a wedding anniversary or birthday, or indeed if you are on honeymoon – '*do not disturb*' notices are available in every cabin and are frequently in use!

Cabins on board ship vary enormously – the cheaper ones being lower down and the larger, more expensive ones on the upper decks, often having balconies. Balconies are not available for cabins nearer the water level, for obvious reasons! Wellingtons are not provided, and a balcony door left open near to sea level could easily cause an emergency situation!

If it is not an indelicate question, what do you require your cabin for? If the answer is merely to sleep in, then why not consider an inside cabin? That is a cabin without a window, and this can be considerably cheaper. All still have private facilities, and at night you'll still have the same effect as those outside cabins with windows – it will be dark!

Bear in mind that, except for balcony doors higher up the ship, windows on ships do not open – the earlier comment about Wellingtons applies here – so if you are lower down the ship all you get through your window is light! Your destination may dictate to you somewhat in this decision – a trip to Norway and the midnight sun in June, where it stays light all night, may be a deciding factor. However, there is little to see at night on a voyage across the Atlantic.

It is also worth remembering that if you are a slightly nervous first time sailor and unsure as to whether you will find your sea legs early in the cruise, in lumpy seas the ship is more stable the lower down you have your cabin, and also towards the centre of the ship.

Where your cabin is situated in the ship does not affect you in any other way when you are on board. You still eat in the same restaurant and you go to the same shows, use the same sun beds and walk on the same decks. The one exception to this is if you have chosen a 'class ship', as with the *Queen Elizabeth 2*, where your cabin grade dictates which dining room you use. However, even on her the other facilities on board are for everybody's use.

* * * * *

OK – so you have decided where to go, what date you want to sail and which cabin you would prefer. You have also accepted a quotation from a cruise club. You will now be asked for a deposit and to arrange your insurance. Your passports must be valid and have a minimum of six months to run following the *end* of your cruise, and depending on the ports you will visit, you may require a visa, but the cruise company will advise you on this subject. The outstanding balance of the cost of the cruise will be required approximately eight weeks before your date of departure.

Injections! Not so important if you're going some-where like the Fjords, but well worth considering if you are planning a trip further afield – or even further afloat! I keep my typhoid, tetanus, poliomyelitis and hepatitis injections up to date, not because there is any danger on board, but because I may be exposed to infection when going ashore in port. Food and drinks on board are hygienically prepared – the same may not be so true of that dark, romantic little restaurant you may visit in – wherever!

If you are going on a cruise to an affected region, a Yellow Fever vaccination may also be a requirement – not free on the NHS, it is, however, value for money as the certificate lasts for ten years – long enough for you to have many cruises under your ever-expanding belt before it needs renewing!

Another facet of cruising is late booking, and here I know of people who *never* book far in advance. If you are able to go at a few days' notice, the discounts you can obtain can be really substantial. You may not get the exact cabin you would choose, but the reduced cost of the cruise will more than amply compensate you for this.

Once 'into' cruising, keep your passport and injections current and your suitcases handy, for like most people you have met on this cruise, you will probably get hooked on cruising too and the bargains that will surely plop through your letter box from the cruise clubs will prove hard to resist.

Only once have I ever met a 'never again' first time cruiser, who was also upset about her shore based holidays – she obviously gained *her* holiday enjoyment from complaining!

* * * * *

And here we come to the end of probably the most boring chapter in this book, but equally one of the most important. Choose the right cruise and you'll have a fabulous time – and once you are on your first cruise, or even when you have arrived home after it, don't forget to join that company's loyalty club. Membership will gain you entrance to a cocktail party on board with the Captain and his Officers, and to a special excursion during your cruise. Sometimes it also entitles you to further discounts off your next cruise with the same company, and, of course, to discounts in the shops on board – shops? Of course there are!

And now you'll have to excuse me, as I'm off to pack for the next cruise. Where did I put the kitchen sink? Don't forget to say 'Hi' when you see me on board! Have a great time on whatever cruise you decide take – but be warned, if it's your first, I doubt very much that it'll be your last.

Patricia Carlton

PATRICIA CARLTON
2005

Oh! PS – I forgot to mention World Cruises.

These leave Southampton early in January and return in April, having circumnavigated the globe... as far as I can see the only stress connected with cruising is the major decision of which way to go... West through the Panama and the Pacific, or East through the Suez and the Indian

Ocean. Can you imagine a better way to pass the worst of the English winter? The decisions connected to cruising are indeed far from simple... but have fun making them!

PPS – Congratulations!

You are now an Honorary Pollywog. Why not join me in my next book when, on the **Queen Elizabeth 2** we'll cross the Equator and you'll become an Honorary Shellback.

See you on board!

POLLYWOGS
and
SHELLBACKS
Go Tropical

Having read this book you are now an experienced cruise passenger, even though you may not yet have set foot afloat.

As you now know, the delights of the Mediterranean are many and you've visited some of my favourites but, if you can spare more than a fortnight, what about venturing further afield on your next voyage?

Pollywogs and Shellbacks Go Tropical is at this moment being written and is due for publication in 2006. In it you'll be on board the *Queen Elizabeth 2*. She's probably the most famous ship in the world: you can enjoy doing the Heritage Tour on board and visit the Bridge from where the crew keep watch safely over you whilst you enjoy your holiday. Attend the 'Crossing the Line' ceremony when all Pollywogs on board will become Shellbacks.

You will visit such exciting places as Dakar in Senegal; experience the peace and serenity of the vast sand dunes in Namibia; watch the magical sight as Table Mountain comes into view as the *Queen Elizabeth 2* enters Cape Town harbour, and enjoy crossing the Indian Ocean to Mauritius. Find out why the French were angry as we arrived at St. Helena and meet the Red-Toed-Sunbather-Bird.

Come sail with me and enjoy another relaxing cruise.
I hope to see you on board and don't forget to say Hello!

PLANKTON BOOKS
Manesty, Weydown Road, Haslemere, Surrey GU27 1DR

Cruise Options are delighted to have been given the opportunity to sponsor Patricia Carlton's Pollywogs and Shellbacks Afloat.

Patricia has been a valued client of Cruise Options for a number of years and we would be delighted to offer the same exceptional service and value to all her readers.

Call Cruise Options now to discover our best possible rates with all the major cruise lines.

Jubilee Lodge, Canning Road, Southport, PR9 7SW

Tel: 0870 755 6006
www.cruiseoptions.co.uk

ABTA
39053